I0073962

RUTHLESS
MARKETING
SECRETS
VOLUME ONE

By **T.J. Rohleder**
(a.k.a "The Blue Jeans Millionaire")

Also by T.J. Rohleder:

The Blue Jeans Millionaire
How to Turn Your Kitchen or Spare Bedroom into a Cash Machine
The Black Book of Marketing Secrets (Series)
The Ultimate Wealth-Maker
Four Magical Secrets to Building a Fabulous Fortune
The Ruthless Marketing Attack
How to Get Super Rich in the Opportunity Market
$60,000.00 in 90 Days
How to Start Your Own Million Dollar Business
Fast Track to Riches
Five Secrets That Will Triple Your Profits
Ruthless Copywriting Strategies
25 Direct Mail Success Secrets That Can Make You Rich
Ruthless Marketing
24 Simple and Easy Ways to Get Rich Quick
How to Create a Hot Selling Internet Product in One Day
50 in 50
Secrets of the Blue Jeans Millionaire
Shortcut Secrets to Creating High-Profit Products

Copyright ® MMX Club-20 International.

All rights reserved. No part of this book may be used or reproduced in
any manner whatsoever without the written permission of the Publisher.
Printed in the United States of America. For information address:
Club-20 International, 305 East Main Street, Goessel, Kansas 67053-0198.

FIRST EDITION

ISBN 1-933356-30-8

TABLE OF CONTENTS:

INTRODUCTION: 5

CHAPTER ONE:
Market Domination 7

CHAPTER TWO:
Fundamental Marketing Strategies 31

CHAPTER THREE:
Big Time, Obscene Profits 53

CHAPTER FOUR:
Dispelling the Marketing Fog 85

CHAPTER FIVE:
Putting DRM to Work in MLM 105

CHAPTER SIX:
Relentless, Aggressive Marketing 129

CHAPTER SEVEN:
Magical Marketing Tricks 141

CHAPTER EIGHT:
It's All About the Systems 161

CHAPTER NINE:
Marketing Should Be Fun! 179

CHAPTER TEN:
Marketing The Back-End 183

Introduction:

T.J. Rohleder here! I'm the co-founder of Mid-American Opportunity Research Enterprises, Inc. (M.O.R.E., Inc., for short) in Goessel, Kansas. My friends call me "the Blue Jeans Millionaire." For the last 21 years, I've been making my financial dreams come true in the marketing field. Now, I don't mean to brag, **but over the years my company has grossed more than $110,000,000 using the methods, tips, and secrets that we've learned and put into play over the years** — secrets that let my wife and I parlay $300 into a huge fortune. No $300,000: I'm talking *three hundred bucks*, the money we got from selling off an old, broken-down carpet-cleaning van. The fact that we took $300 and built it into a financial empire ought to tell you something — if you'll do a little math, you'll see we multiplied our original investment by almost 370,000 times (366,667, to be precise).

So how did we do that? The short answer is this: We mixed a little luck, a heaping helping of hard work, and the rigorous application of those secrets I mentioned in the previous paragraph. And you know what? **I'll happily share every secret I know with you.** That's why I've decided to create this series, the first volume of which you're holding in your hands right now.

By now, you might be scratching your head a little. After all, the title of this book is *Ruthless Marketing Secrets, Volume I* — and if I really *were* practicing ruthless marketing, why would I share my secrets with you, even for a price? Wouldn't it be more ruthless, and more logical, to keep everything to myself? In fact, wouldn't it be smarter to just crush potential competitors before they even got started?

Heck no, and here's why. First of all, I believe the more the merrier. **Competition sharpens everyone's abilities, keeps the**

marketplace jumping, and proves that the market I'm in is still vibrant. Second, I make a significant portion of my money by helping people just like you, and **I honestly believe that by showing you these things, I'm enriching both of us.** I hold the opinion that there's abundance in the marketplace out there, and that there's a big enough pie for us all. And hey, the fact is that you probably won't end up working the exact same market as I do — but if you do, welcome to the club! There's plenty of room for a serious marketer.

This book, and the ones that will follow, are based on a series of weekly Masters of Marketing conference calls that a number of my colleagues and I have been enjoying together for years. The participants in these calls included various members of our One Hundred Million Dollar Roundtable and our Board of Governors: marketing experts like as Eric Bechtold, Alan R. Bechtold, Jeff Gardner, and Chris Hollinger — and of course Chris Lakey, our Director of Marketing, and I participated in each one. We'll hear from all these experts and more in subsequent volumes.

Ready to get ruthless? If so, turn the page, and let's get cracking!

CHAPTER ONE

Market Domination

An important step in any successful ruthless marketing strategy is planning out how you can dominate your marketplace. You don't have to absolutely crush the competition (though that never hurts), but you do need to find a way to climb to the top of that market and become king of the mountain. In this chapter, I'll outline three aspects of the topic:

1. How to dominate any market... period.

2. How to turn any information into irresistible marketing.

3. How to quickly create stunning information products.

Let's dive right in, shall we?

How to Dominate a Market

To really dominate a market, you need to start with a niche: a specialty market or submarket. Look for something that you enjoy doing already — anything, even adult subjects. Obviously, you can turn sex into money; we've seen the pornography industry do this for years. And there are more non-offensive ways to do, it, too: dating sites, marital advice, counseling, different kinds of couples coaching. You don't even have to be licensed to do that, if that's what you like doing. The point is, be very careful what you wish for, because it's got to be something that you love doing and that you're never going to get too tired of. And let's be honest, we all get tired; as you get older, some things are harder to do 24/7, and you might not be able to maintain your passion for something that you've been doing for a while. **So you've got to be careful that you pick a niche that you're passionate about.**

I deal with clients one-on-one all the time, so I hear the same thing over and over again... and I've got to tell you, it surprises me. Probably 87% of the customers I talk to want to get into the Internet marketing business or sell information about Internet marketing or about marketing in general. While I'm all about information publishing, I have to point out to these people that, first of all, this is a crowded business now. It seems like every three days there are 200 new superstars booming on the Internet, and that may lead a lot of people to believe, "Well, obviously it's easy, and I want to break in." **But, honestly, it's tough.** It's tough to break into any niche, any interest.

You've got to establish yourself as an expert: That's the key to dominating a market. But how do you do that if you're brand-spanking new to marketing? You're not an expert *yet*, are you? Or are you? The fact is, if you find something you're already interested in and know something about, you *are* already an expert. That's something that most people don't realize: if you've been collecting thimbles for six months, you're an expert to someone who just started. You know more than they do. Now, thimble collecting isn't a real profitable hobby. But if you want to get into the Internet marketing business, here's how I see so many newcomers doing it. **This is the magic key: they focus on a niche that they're interested in, applying the stuff they're learning about Internet marketing to that niche, teaching people what they know about Internet marketing.** A lot of people simply don't understand the extent of what you can do with technology these days. In a recent conversation with a fellow marketer, she mentioned that she was talking to a bunch of small business owners who aren't Internet marketing experts, and was telling them about how she's got classes that they can call in and listen to on the phone. And they went, "You mean you can hold seminars on the phone?"

That just blows my mind. In the Internet marketing field, we've been doing that since the early 1990s! **But there are whole segments of businesses that don't know about phone seminars.** Giving away an eBook is new to them, too... and that's certainly not new anymore. It's one of the quickest, easiest things you can learn about and carry over into another area, and most people don't know a thing about it. At that point, if you have some knowledge to it, you've suddenly become the expert.

Here's a great example: a fellow named Joe Polish. This guy specialized in carpet cleaning. He took what he knew and loved about marketing to that arena, and now he's the Mr. Multi-Bajillionaire Super Marketing Expert every carpet cleaner in the world turns to when they want to learn about marketing. In that small circle he's a household name — and he's making tons of money without ever leaving that circle. **Most business people can profit by learning the secrets of marketing:** needlecrafters, bead workers, automotive mechanics, hairdressers, antique dealers. I can't believe how few antique dealers know how to market, for example. All you've got to do is study the things I'll teach you in this book, and in all the other products we produce here at M.O.R.E., Inc., and our Direct-Response Marketing Network (DRN).

But if you were to start looking in the Yellow Pages and newspapers, you'd notice that in every one of those arenas I just mentioned, **hardly anyone is using those techniques.** They go by the standard methods; but if you want to make an impression, you can't just follow the crowd. **You need to establish yourself as an expert in a niche.** A fellow named Brad Fallon is a good example. This guy is the King of Search Engine Optimization among Internet marketers. So how did he get to become king? Well, he started a website selling wedding favors, of all things. That's the stuff you set out for wedding guests; the little gifts you give them for coming, or the gifts you give to your bridesmaids. Sounds like an impossible niche, right?

Well, that's the one thing his wife loved: putting together and catering weddings. So they started selling wedding favors. And they also sell themed stuff; for example, stuff for setting up a beach wedding. Coupled with search engine optimization, this took them to the $10,000,000-a-year mark. Then he took what he learned and turned that into a "How I Did This…" course for his site. That's how he came to the attention of the Internet marketing world — unknown at first, but with solid credentials behind him.

Do you see the carryover there, and how it works? Most people don't. That's why so many people shake their heads and say, "Why would I waste my time selling 'How To Market Your Business' to beekeepers, just because I love bees?" But why shouldn't you? You understand that market. You understand the customer. You may find that you never have to leave that niche; but if you decide to, **all you need to do is apply many of the same strategies you already know to the new market.**

Perry Marshall is an expert in Pay Per Click strategies. He teaches you to find a niche you can dominate, then after you've achieved that domination — after you've established your foothold there as an expert with customers and great cash flow — you slowly start expanding your niche. **"Expand your universe,"** as he says. That's exactly what he did. He became the King of Pay Per Click. Now he teaches copywriting. He's starting to bring in other elements of marketing and stuff and expand his universe. It just makes sense, since he's made a name for himself and he's got the customers. This is the way that many marketers expand their empires. As the money starts flowing in, and you start developing some customers and you start building your niche, you also gain confidence that you don't have in the very beginning. **With that confidence comes a willingness to try some new things and to expand a little more,** since you're more confident working within your own realm. Now you've got the confidence to march right into a broader arena. That broader arena may be as simple as going from beekeepers to dealing with the larger manufacturing companies as a consultant. It might be adding marketing tools for stores to help them sell more health food products like honey. **But now you're expanding outward; there's still a hook.**

That's one way to dominate any market: **start with a niche that *needs* to be dominated.** There are still hundreds of thousands of them waiting for that expert to come along. Let's say you're into doll collecting. If there's already somebody there or there's quite a bit of information about it, you want to drill downward a little to find a smaller "sub-niche." A sub-niche may involve specializing only in a certain type of doll, or doll clothing, even collectible vintage dolls clothing. Then you might expand to being the expert at preserving collectibles of all types.

And remember, the **Internet has created even more markets, and in fact we're getting smaller niches within niches.** It's happening online because of the cost of setting up that old-fashioned brick-and-mortar store, and the limitations of how far out from the store you can market. Let's say you start out thinking you'd better open a pet store. But already there are three pet stores in town, and now you're competing with all of them in that locality. Online, though, you can open a store that sells nothing but designer leashes for pet geckos and probably find enough customers to make a little money. I'm not going to say it would earn you a living, but I'll bet you could make enough to keep the site open.

I may be getting a little ridiculous here, but that's the difference between the sub-niches and the niches in a nutshell. For example, there are websites that actually sell clothing just for daschunds. Now, that's getting real nichey. Before, the only hope you had of selling anything like that would be manufacturing them yourself and hopefully getting stores to buy them, as one item they'd sell among many. But now you can literally open up a pet store and call it "My Favorite Daschund." It's just incredible.

One thing you want to do when looking to dominate your market is to **look for competition. You do *not* want to drill down to a sub-niche where there's no competition.** That's a warning signal that indicates there's also no money in that niche; it's equivalent to hanging around a place at night where there's light and there are all these moths around. You might say, "Hey, let's go where there aren't any moths." Do that, though, and you can't see — the only place where there aren't any moths is where there's no light. Well, that's great, but you can't see what you're doing. Same thing here. **If there's no competition, it's because no one is buying anything.**

Very rarely will you find an arena where there isn't already somebody there. That's proof that there's money there. But the key is, how big are they? What are they doing to attract the money? **It's still so easy to beat these people; most don't understand real direct marketing principles.** I mentioned earlier that an amazing number of niches are open; you can type the wildest stuff into an Internet search engine and see 10,000 websites supporting it. It just amazes me. But when you start looking at the websites, you'll find that very rarely are there many of them actually selling a lot of stuff. And if they are actually selling, they're doing it wrong! It's so easy to beat five competitors in a little sub-niche than it is one giant established Amazon.com.

On the other hand, maybe you could just be an affiliate and sell books about a topic — drill down into a sub-niche and review those books, really read them and bring them to people's attention, and make them available for them to buy. It's a lot easier that way. But in any case, **what you want to do first is study your competition. This is the scary part: you want to become a customer of any competitor.** I see so many people cringe when I mention this. Why? Because they think, "Oh, I'm going to have to buy stuff from my competitor? I don't want to give them my money!" Well, you're giving them money in return for valuable market research. There's no other way to do it. Just look at it this way: **it's legal espionage.** And it's actually moral and ethical, too. A while back I heard about a store that was doing espionage on another store. The guy went into the store and stood there with a notebook writing stuff down, and they started to recognize who he was and kicked him out! They can't do that online.

In his book *Made In America*, the late Sam Walton claimed that he was thrown out of more K-Mart stores than any other person in the whole world. Today, he could just study the K-Mart website. He could buy a few things and see how they follow through. Buy them in his wife's name, so they don't recognize the "Sam" in front of Walton, have them ordered to another post office box somewhere where they don't know it's his, and watch the process. Do they include upsell offers or additional offers in the package when they send it? Does it come quickly? Did they call to verify? Is there email follow-up? You can learn all these things by buying from a competitor. **You study them, and then you start offering ways to improve upon the things you notice that you could do better or**

differently. Again, this is the benefit of working in an area you're already excited about, because in a sense you are your own customer!

At M.O.R.E., Inc., we're on a mission to expand what we've been doing since 1988 and reach a much wider audience. **One of the reasons we feel like we *can* do this is because we started within our niche as customers.** Since then we've mastered it; we intimately know everything there is to know about selling business opportunities, and all of the psychographics that go into that particular subject matter, so now we're taking all that we've learned and we're expanding it to a larger market.

That's why I brought up the subject of confidence a little bit ago. A lot of people are hesitant and let fear control them, in what our friend Ken Pedersen calls "vapor lock." But that changes when you get out there, work within a niche, and do all these things I've been talking about here. You start the cash register ringing, you get to know your customers, you start looking at other things that they need — and then you develop enough confidence that you can move into a broader market.

Most of our customers are very ambitious people; they want to make millions of dollars. Well, let me tell you, **the niche doesn't have to be that big to make millions.** A second point is that with confidence, knowledge and experience comes the ability to take things to much higher level, a level you can only imagine when you're first getting started. Another advantage of doing it for a while on a smaller scale with a niche is that you also gather resources and suppliers you can count on, people who are now behind you and working with you so that as you expand, you're not looking for the resources and suppliers; you've already got them. All you've got to do is add zeroes to the numbers they're producing. That makes it much easier to expand.

But what are you going to sell people? **Well, I'm a big fan of information marketing, because of the profit margin.** Take Brad Fallon, the fellow selling the wedding favors; he does about $1.2 million a month. Most people reading this are probably thinking, "Wow, a million two a month... I'd be happy as a lark." He doesn't clear that; the markup on that stuff can't be huge, and he's got to battle others who supply the same market. So what if he's number one? That doesn't help if you've got an 8% markup profit when all is said and done. So yes, he makes probably a fine living selling those wedding favors, but then he turned around and started selling his courses on how he did it, and started making millions more with virtually no cost. Then he teamed up with some other people and started this huge thing called Stomper Net that you've got to pay $900 a month to get into, and he just launched a video/audio sharing service that's supposedly competing with YouTube. The guy is going nuts now! **Just like him, you need to keep expanding and expanding and expanding.**

Now, I don't want anybody reading this to think that this is *precisely* how you've got to go. **What's cool is, there's no limit to how far you can go, and there's no one telling you to go beyond where you're comfortable.** So you're making $100,000 and you're happy, stay where you're at! **Look, knowledge really can make all the difference in the world.** It's only when you learn all the fine points of marketing that you can get to the point of looking at things differently. Now you can see all of these competitors and say, "Oh, we can beat him. We can beat that one, too." It gives you the ability to see what people are doing right, but it also lets you see how many people are out there doing it wrong. You've got the experience now. You can spot what's good and what's not, what's working and what isn't. You start knowing in your gut that if you can just find a way to make deliveries arrive at people's doorsteps a day earlier, you've nailed this thing. That's what they want. That's what they'll respond to.

Another thing: just starting out, there are some advantages. And this is another one where people start slapping their foreheads when I mention it — but the truth is, if you're starting out on your kitchen table with a phone and a post office box, **you can compete against major corporations in one area where I *know* they can never beat you at: personal contact.** You're in touch with the customers. If you don't have customer support and a long track record yet, how about this? "If you call my office, you get me." You don't tell them it's because you're so small and new at this, but you can still turn it into a plus. Sure, maybe you can only handle 50, 100, or 200 clients that way... maybe 500 or 1,000, depending on your business. There will be a limit, but man, milk it for all it's worth while that's where you're stuck, because the big guys just can't compete with that. They can't get on the phone with customers themselves every day; they have to have a staff. They've built it too far beyond that. **So right off the bat, you focus on what you can compete with and actually win.** And believe me, there are people who will actually pay you more money than they'd pay a larger competitor because of that.

Another area where a smaller company can compete is the fact that, **because they don't have all the overhead expenses that we have, they can make more money with less percentage of a response than we can.** We tell this to people who are getting involved in our marketplace all the time. First of all, we like competition. We think it's good for the marketplace. We encourage it. Well, starting out, they have all kinds of advantages that we don't have, because our response rates have to be so much higher just to cover our basic overhead expenses, let alone make a profit. We compare it to the ocean, when you have a small boat versus a big huge ship. The small boat can go in circles around that big ship. It's going to take forever to get that big ship turned around. The big ship can carry a lot more, but the small one can make eight trips in the same amount of time. That small has plenty of advantages boat has in certain waters.

Think about that, and apply it to a cool sub-niche you're excited about. **Information products are a great example, since they have the highest markup.** But it takes a time to put them together. **Here's what you do if you want to start immediately: go to Clickbank.com and become an affiliate marketer.** Start searching for items that fit your sub-niche; these are programs that pay you a percentage on what you sell. They'll get you started and make you some sales. They even give you the sales material to present to the people so that you can study how it's working, and then tweak it. **You don't have to start from scratch. But then, meanwhile, you start working on your own unique information products: eBooks, newsletters, audios, videos.** And when you're working in all those different media, they allow you to do it online. This enables you to sell stuff digitally at no cost to you. You can also take the same product and make them available on CD or DVD or in print, offering multiple versions of just one product. I hope you realize that what I'm handing you here is not only how to get started, but how to get started *quickly*.

Achieving Irresistible Marketing

Start playing with what I've already showed you right now, so you're already honing your marketing chops while you're creating your first unique product. There are exceptions to every rule, but in my mind **the basic rule is that you're *really* going to get ahead when you have your own unique products to sell.** That leads us into the next step, because once you've got your product you have complete control over the market. You can control the price. You can control your profit margin. But there's even a better reason, in my mind, for having your own information products — and that's **because you can turn them into irresistible marketing.** That's when it really starts getting interesting.

It's really simple. Let's say you come up with a 140-page eBook you're going to sell, or you record a 60-minute CD. You take snippets out and make points with them and say, "This is on page so-and-so." For example, pull out two paragraphs and say, "The rest of this is on page 13." And take two more paragraphs and say, "For the rest of this tip, look at page 72." You can do the same thing with audio. You can play an audio clip and say, "This is just five minutes into the CD." **The information itself becomes your marketing material;** you almost don't need a sales letter when you use this technique the right way. It's just something to lead in and get people's interest, and then slam them with these hot information tips that don't go all the way, but are still great as they are.

If it's free and it's got valuable information in it, people will read it if it's 10 pages or 100. **Here's the key: Notice that I said to put your very *best* information in there.** So many people think, "Hey, I'm giving this stuff away. I don't want to give away the best material." Don't tell that to the movie industry! I don't think I've ever seen a movie trailer yet that didn't have 90% of the whole movie's production budget poured into the clip. And, as I've often noticed (and I bet you have, too), sometimes those are the only good scenes in the movie! What does that do? It drives people to the theater.

So give them your very best right there in the freebie, right up front. **Always try to over-deliver; you don't want to give them junk.** And if it's repeated in the material itself, that just underscores the fact that they made a wise decision buying from you.

When you give this stuff away on the Web, the cool thing is

that you're providing people with the most popular thing sought after on the Internet: **FREE information!** And what you do is say, "Hey, you can download this free eBook." This is really powerful. "Download this free report or this free eBook. All we need is your email address and your name, so we can send it to you." See, a lot of people just put links where you can download it; but I say, send them the link in an email. **That way you have to have their email address and name, so now you're building a list.** What you do next is email the list once a week with updates and additional little nuggets from your information pieces, news about new products you're working on; and in every other email, sometimes every third one, offer something for sale. This is where those Clickbank products can come back into play. While you're working on your next product, offer them one or two. **This is the perfect way to build up a list of people who are interested and already look up to you as an expert, and are now building a relationship with you.**

A while back, Chris Lakey and I were working on a new business plan. We were running some numbers and setting some goals, and our initial goal was to bring in 1,200 people per week, people who are going to raise their hand, initially, to send for a free offer. We figured that at the end of a year, that would be 50,000+ new prospects. And so we started to talk about all the different things we could offer to those people. We could offer them this, we could create this for them, we could do this for them. **People don't realize that that's how millions of dollars are being made.**

The thing that we're talking about here — building a mailing list, finding people who are interested in what you sell, and then trying to find as many other kinds of products and services to offer those people as possible — is part of trying to develop a relationship with them. **It sounds simple, and it *is* simple. It's not always easy to do, though, and sometimes it**

takes years to really master it. And yet, this is the basis of making the millions of dollars that I know you want to make.

It's a well-known fact that **it's a lot easier to find more people than it is to create a new product.** A new product is either going to be a hit or a miss. But when you keep bringing new people on board, every product you already have is new to them. **You build a buyer list, so you've got a list of people who trust you and know you, and you keep bringing new ones on.** There's nothing more fun than having a list of 50,000 customers when you've got a new product to announce, especially when they've already bought from you and they trust and know you. You drop a new product on their lap and they go crazy. I've seen Internet marketers pull their servers down because people came crashing to them so quickly wanting a product, just because they had a nice big responsive list. **It's all about the list, your relationship with it, and your understanding of it.**

Remember: **you need to get on the other side of the cash register, be objective and learn how your customers think.** Learn how they think, what they obsess about, what they truly want. You need to buy from all of your competitors so that you get a real feeling for the marketplace, what's out there, who's selling what, and what's working the best. That's what makes success happen.

Creating Information Products

So, how do you create those information products that sell so well? By now, you may be thinking, "Well, that would be great if I knew how to write, or if I *liked* to write." Most people shudder at the thought of writing; it's almost like public speaking. But you don't have to write to create information products. You do need to map out an outline and maybe answer some questions, but I believe everybody has that capability.

In fact, **answering questions is often the very easiest way to create an information product: just ask the people in your market what they want.** There are some systems online you can use to ask your customers to take a survey — or you can just call ten of your clients and say, "Hey, what's the one question you most need answered in your business?" You might be surprised at the results. If you get 10 questions and answer them with three or four paragraphs apiece, you'll end up with a lot of information. Or invite an expert on board, and ask them those questions and record it; viola, you've got an information product! You could also have that transcribed. Now, if you have a 60-90 minute recording transcribed, that translates to a little more than 25-50 single-spaced pages. Ninety minutes can be almost a 75-page eBook. But whatever you do, edit it! A lot of guys crank out these eBooks that are nothing but transcriptions, and nobody likes to read a transcription. That worked for a while, but it's getting old. **All you've got to do is clean it up, get out the uhs, ands, and ahs. You can leave it in Q&A format if you want, but it's really better if you can work it to look more like a paragraph or an actual chapter.**

Now, here's something really cool: **Ask experts to contribute a chapter to a book.** There's a fellow named Willie Crawford who's very well-known in the marketing world. He released an eBook a while back that I thought was really cool. He had 19 experts and himself each write a chapter, detailing their own unique way that someone could easily start generating part-time money at a rate of $100 a day. We're not talking about millions here; we're not talking about getting rich online. Just $100 a day. That's three grand a month. To the average middle-class person looking to start their own business, that's business capital. That's life-changing, a foundation to build on.

Willie ended up with 20 chapters that worked out as a 270-

page eBook, and he sold it for $27 a copy. And it's digital! **Other people did all the work; he wrote one chapter.** When people bought the book, they could resell it; **it came with full resale rights.** So he got other people distributing his chapter in that book, and he gave them 100% of the $27. Well, who could refuse to buy the whole thing then? **He collected 52,000 new names for his list in a week.** And here's the other cool thing: when you bought the $27 eBook, up popped an offer before you went to download the book to add $9 to your order and get Willie Crawford's 17-page eBook about how he got those 52,000 names!

This just shows you how that **when you're selling information products, you can create money out of thin air** — sometimes in weeks or days. Another thing is, **finding experts is pretty simple.** They're on websites; some of them are on your competitors' websites. Why not interview a competitor? At least an indirect competitor — someone not directly competing, but someone in your niche. Take the doll clothing example; go find some companies that sell Barbie clothes and find out who their CEO or resident expert is, and interview them. You can also look at press releases online. Any time you go to a website, there's always a "Contact Us" page on the site, or a "Press Room." Go into the Press Room online, and you'll find every press release that company has released. Right there on those press releases is the name of the person to contact for interviews. This is a great way to find experts to interview and to create your quickie eBook to build a list.

When all else fails, I tell people, "Go hire a ghostwriter." There's a site called elance.com where you can go post a bid and say something like, "I'm willing to pay $200 for someone to write me an eBook on this subject. Will provide the outline." In fact, you can actually safely say $500 or $1,000 because what will happen is, all these people who write books under contract on elance will come back and say, "I'll do it for $800. I'll do it for $700." They underbid each other. What you do is just check out their references, sample works, feedback, and what have you.

Now, I'm not telling you to take the lowest bid. You might pick the middle bid, because if they've got a fairly decent turn-around time and a good record, the mid-price range is usually the guy that's going to do the best job. The higher-priced ones are going to do a good job, but they're probably going to be out-priced. After all, you want to keep your budget as low as you can. So I like to trim it down. Every time you go below the middle is when you start running into hit-or-miss situations. But the truth is, **I've been shocked at the number of good writers who are more than willing to take on work for dirt-cheap prices,** compared to ghostwriters you find elsewhere. You'll find that some of those people charge exorbitant rates, and yet we've gone on elance and found some very talented people for pennies on the dollar. elance is a great resource for all kinds of things, in fact.

Getting back to ClickBank for a moment, it offers a great way to get started if you don't want to go the elance route. **They've got more than 10,000 products, and you can instantly become an affiliate.** My suggestion is to go pick out some products that you like, ones that are very nichey, and instead of just advertising their affiliate link, go spend ten bucks at Godaddy.com, register a domain name, and make it something unique. And then you can actually give someone the impression they're going to a site that's owned by you, even though all they're doing is going through an affiliate re-direct.

You can make money with all kinds of affiliate programs on ClickBank, and elance is good for finding all kinds of stuff dirt-cheap. I don't know if it's because of all the competition or if people just aren't in tune to what they should be or could be charging, but **you can easily find people to re-write your audio products into text.** If you've recorded an interview, you can find people to re-write that material and make it more like a book, instead of it sounding like it's the spoken word. You can find ghostwriters who will take your topic and write it, charging you by the page. **There are all kinds of things you can do on elance to find any of those kinds of services.** It's a great place to find transcriptionists, too, to take that audio recording of an interview with an expert and turn it into the raw material that you're going to create a book from. This can all be done fairly quickly. When my friend Alan Bechtold was promoting his Franklin Guild, he wanted to do a free report; so he decided, "Let's just hold a teleconference call." They recorded the teleconference call two weeks before they were going to be at an Internet marketing event where they wanted to hand out the printed report.

So they had it transcribed and edited, sent it over to the Kinko's in San Francisco closest to where this conference was, and the printed report was waiting for them when they got there. In two weeks they had a printed book! That's just incredible. **Technology has made it possible for the little guy to do so many things and to make money through all these inexpensive high-tech tools.** It's such an exciting time to be alive! And I've got to tell you, it just gets more exciting all the time. Consider podcasting: it's *another* way to create content. Podcasting is when you do your recording and put it out on the Internet so people can listen to it on their iPods and play it on the computer. **Podcasting has proven to be very attractive to the search engines.** A lot of people use them for no other reason than to attract tons of people to websites and build an audience, and then the podcast itself becomes your marketing *and* the product. Save the recordings, and what have you got now? A CD. Add PowerPoint, and you've got a DVD. **You've created new versions of the same product.**

You can even make a conference call into an eBook and then make the eBook available for free, digitally. People do this all the time. And then they tell you, "But for just $19.95, we'll send you the original recording of the call on CD *and* a printed book." Even though it's free to get the book, you'll get up to 20% of the people saying, "I'd rather read it on the john," or, "I'd rather have the CD to listen to in the car." And they'll actually order it. **Same event, three different products.**

I mentioned Joe Polish earlier. Twelve years ago I bought one of Joe's products; back then it was a cassette tape. I thought it was so cool! All it consisted of was Joe and a friend who were driving in Joe's car for three hours on their way to seminar, so they decided they were going to create an information product while they were driving! So it's got all the noise in the background from the semis passing them and all the road noise, and it was done on the cheapest little handheld recorder. But they produced this program and sold it by making a big deal of the fact that by listening in, you're like a fly on the wall. You can just see it: this inner-circle conversation between two expert marketers trapped in their vehicle for three hours. What else are they going to do but talk shop? If they were doing it now, they could have done a live call. They could have hooked up via their cell phones into a teleconference system, and had people paying even more for immediate access. "Hey, while we're driving, here's how many hours we're going to be in the car and, hey, no matter what we're talking about, whether it's sports or business or anything, you're going to just be listening in."

I know several marketers now who are starting to do things like that. While driving to a conference they will actually post to their blogs at local coffee shops along the way. Just make a stop, grab some coffee, update my blog. "Well, here's what we were talking about on the way…" It's just amazing! **There are so many tools out there now.** We take for granted today what Joe

Polish didn't have access to back then. We've got so many more opportunities to make money now, especially in information publishing and marketing, where the average person can do so much more with so much less equipment or money than it would have taken 10 years ago to do the same — if it was even possible 10 years ago. And that's an important point. People will tell me, "How can you still sell information when there's so much of it free on the Web?" **Well, I want to see *more* of it free on the Web, and I'll tell you why: it overwhelms people.** They're confused and lost, trying to find exactly the information they need, and they'll happily pay you to go get that free information. **There's tons of it out there you can get and reuse legally.** This is another way that you don't have to write a thing; it's all out there. You just want to watch out for copyrights, of course. Just because it's on the web doesn't mean you can use it. But press releases and white papers? This is all stuff that's issued not only for public consumption, but because they hope you'll publish it and redistribute it.

There are a lot of competitors out there, too, and that's a positive thing — never a negative thing. Don't look at it that way. One of the ideas that keeps recurring in this business is that too many people focus on the obstacles to business rather than the outcomes. They look at all of the competition as an obstacle rather than an opportunity. But it's not. **It proves that there's a marketplace that's already established for whatever you want to sell.** Again, we believe that competition is a good thing; it should never be feared. Not only does it make this game fun, it's the best model in the world to study to see what you should or shouldn't be doing with your own business. I order tons of products from what most people would consider my competitors. And most of the time I don't order it because I want the information; **I order it to study the process they use to a) get me to order it and b) deliver it to me and then c) follow it up.**

I've got this really sharp marketer right now who's been after me. I know I'm going to eventually respond to her, but I'm holding back until I get that final notice letter, because I'm saving up all of her different sequential mailings. Hey, it's market research! I've bought many an information marketing product where I learned much more from the process than from the product. That's a lesson for everybody reading this. You can learn a lot not just by buying a product, but by receiving the sales material. **There's a lot of research to be had out there by analyzing not only the products and services being offered, but the whole selling process.** Get on people's lead lists, request information, and then study it and think about it like a marketer instead of a consumer, and you'll learn a lot about how to sell your own stuff.

It's all about the marketer's mindset. Again, you've got to get on the other side of the cash register. **You've got to start thinking like a marketer.** A quick warning, though: it can become highly addictive. Some of us can't even go to a restaurant anymore without commenting on the lousy menu, talking about how they didn't present that meal the right way, or how they missed an opportunity to capture their name as they left. Another side effect is that sure does bother your spouse or your significant other. And guests — someone goes out to eat with you, and you're griping about how the waiter didn't even ask you for your email address.

You can get quite an education out of other people's sales material. You see so many bad TV commercials and direct-mail pieces and Internet stuff out there, and that's why we're not afraid of competition: **because 99% of it doesn't know what it's doing!** That's why it's so easy to dominate a niche or sub-niche, especially when you're starting out with a brand new card-table business. Like I said, there are a few niches that are taken, like books. I hate to hand it all to them, but let's assume that between Amazon, Barnes & Noble, Books A Million and a few others, they've pretty much got that sewed up. But there are other book niches. There are rare book collectors; there are First Edition book collectors; there are signed book collectors. You've got to drill down a little more to a smaller sub-niche, and now it's possible to dominate it. Now, exploitable niches may not be as obvious as you might think. For example, many people who think of information marketing only think about books, whereas **I hope I've made it clear that the field also includes teleseminars, seminars, workshops, eBooks, CDs, DVDs, online video, and podcasting — and now there's vodcasting.** That's the video equivalent of podcasting, where it's video for the iPod. There are new iPods that now show video as well as audio.

As technology evolves, there will be all kinds of newer and more powerful ways to sell information. **The market is going to increasingly belong to the smaller company or individual, because the niches will shrink.** The bigger advertisers are definitely suffering right now, and they will continue to suffer. As a matter of fact, here's something that just recently happened: We've got TiVo, where you can digitally record all your TV shows, and whenever you do that you can fast-forward the commercials. And so I told my wife Eileen, "Someday in the future, you're just going to be able to touch one little button and the commercial is going to be zapped out, and it's going to go to your show again." Well, I just read that the new TiVos have that feature in them. That's because they know that sells TiVos, and they're going to sell TiVos like crazy!

But think about how you'll feel if you're an advertiser paying millions of dollars to advertise, as millions of people get these new TiVos. **The market belongs to the small player now, who because of technology has more power than ever before.** And that's exciting for somebody who's just getting into this! I hear this all the time in relation to Internet marketing: "Am I too late?" Holy crap! You're getting on the pony when it's just starting to go! The drink has just arrived! It's far from over! No, in fact, we're just now getting in the area where we've gone through the growing pains of the 2000 dot-com bust. **The survivors are thriving, and now we know what doesn't work.** We've tried a model that failed miserably, so nobody's going there right now; and I'm glad to see that.

I happen to think that every marketer should be selling information products. **It doesn't matter what business you're in, you should be selling information products to niche markets.** I hope this chapter has provided you with a blueprint on how to do it. The thing to do now is to just get out there and start: find the niche markets that interest you the most, see what those people want, what they're looking for, and what their biggest problems are. If you can solve those problems, whether through an eBook, audio programs, CDs, even video podcasts and all the new technology, **then there's a whole lot of money to be made.**

CHAPTER TWO:

Fundamental Marketing Strategies

In this chapter, I've got some very important marketing strategies to share — the kind you should never go into business without taking to heart. **Let's start by taking a look at what I consider one of the most important tools any marketer can use in this confusing, hype-ridden world: honesty.**

It Really Is the Best Policy

This is one of those things that seems to get by so many people: **the truth is 100 times stronger than a lie.** So many new marketers get idea that marketing is all about lying creatively, but that's not marketing at all. That's hype and rip-off. Yet the reason we *believe* it's true is that so much of the marketing we're constantly barraged with is loaded with lies. **Well, you want to cut through the clutter.** That's why honesty is such a powerful tool to use in marketing. **Plus, it lets you sleep at night!**

By being honest, you stand out when above all those other marketing messages. You can really get down to the nitty-gritty, captivate your prospect's interest, and build believability. **Believability turns into sales.** We've got to constantly remind ourselves that prospects may not know you, and even your customers may not trust you fully until you've given them a reason to do so. **The truth is what develops that trust, and it builds a rapport faster than anything I've ever seen.**

I recently saw a powerful example of this in action. It was a promotion by a well-known Internet marketer who sold a system that taught people how to dominate their market niche online through something he called "Mass Control." Now, I'm not going to name him; you'll know who he is if you're in the Internet marketing world, and you'll be familiar with the product, because this thing was blasted all over the Web. The guy is brilliant; **he used a system to sell this, and was teaching his system, the same system he's used to make — get this — more than $23 million in sales online** *in a single 24-hour period*. He broke all records, and he did it for someone else. The system includes posting a series of free videos that are easy to put together and virtually give away the store, teaching people valuable training they need to build their online businesses the right way.

But he also carefully structured things so that it's preparing them for wanting his Mass Control System, which he was selling at $2,000-a-pop when he opened the doors. The trick was to bring your customers up to speed with this free series of videos; or, you could do the same thing with special reports or audios. **The point was to deliver information that actually prepares them for wanting the course, while leaving the doors closed and letting people know it's going to open for only so many hours on a certain date, and then selling out everything you've got at two grand just as he did.**

He even told people while he was doing this that the system he's teaching them is being used on them to get them to want the course. That was the truth; you can see it in the promotion. But what's funny is, midway through his promotion he sent out an email that I thought was completely shocking, and it went like this: "I'm getting a lot of questions about my Mass Control

System. Many of you are obviously interested and eager for the doors to open, and they will be open soon. But one question keeps getting asked over and over again, and I simply have to deal with it here. The question is, "Do I need a list of prospects to make your Mass Control System work?" His answer was, **"Of course you need a list to make it work!** Whatever made you think it could work without one? You need a list to make *any* business work. Anyone who tries to tell you otherwise is fooling themselves and trying to fool you, too, if you buy into it." But he went on to say that, because so many people were asking, his next training video was going to be all **about how he builds his own list, and the steps anyone without a list can follow to build their own easily, cheaply, and quickly.** And then they'll be ready to buy his Mass Control.

What I recommend is that you follow this example. **If you find there's a flaw in any product or service you offer, bring it to the forefront.** There's no such thing as a flawless product; we all know that. So deal with it honestly. If you can, find a way around the problem, just like the man in the example did. He said, "Okay, my product doesn't work without a list." If lots of people are saying, "Oh darn, I need a list!" then show them how to build a list! He sold tons of that product to people who hadn't yet used his system to build a list, because he gave it to them. They knew they were going to be able to, so that knocked that whole objection out the door.

So you want to ask yourself, what objections exist in the mind of anyone who's reading your sales copy or studying your promotion? **Find those objections, and deal with them honestly.** As a matter of fact, the more you put your hand to your mouth and whisper, "By the way, this is something no one else will tell you, but I've got to tell you here," the more powerful that truth will be, and the more endearing you'll be to your list.

Too many people view marketing and selling as if it's lying for a living. Sure, sometimes we try to stretch it as far as we can without lying; but the bottom line is, **marketing is all about differentiation — separating yourself from everybody else.** So if everybody else is hyping it up, you're in a big position to simply tell the truth and be very upfront, very clear with people. It really shocks them, so it cuts right through the clutter. **People are so used to being having things hidden from them that if you just lay it all on the line, you'll win their trust.** They may be a little offended sometimes, but with that being offended also comes the realization that you're a person who won't BS them.

We put out an offer recently that was highly controversial. Before we ran it, we showed our staff what it was first — and several of our key staff members, people who have been with us for a long time, almost begged us not to run it. They told us to be careful with it, because it was a brutally honest promotion. We went ahead and took the risk, and here we are many hundreds of thousands of dollars in pure profits later. We're the ones who knew all along that in this day and age, you do have to shock people. You have to wake them up, you have to snap them out of their little trances, and that's exactly why our promotion was so controversial: because it tells the truth.

Here's another way to get people's attention. We've had promotions where we say, "By the way, if you meet these criteria, this offer is *not* for you. Stop wasting your time. Go find something else to buy." You'll find people tend to have an attitude of, "Well, that's not me!" Even if they do fit those criteria, they're going to dig their heels in and go, "Yeah, right, I'll buy this just to prove you wrong!" In the controversial offer I just referred to, we actually tell people that there's a substantial cost to purchasing the product from us, and they have to meet several qualifications. **In the lead generation phase, where we ask people to raise their hands say they want our report** from us, we tell them right up front that it's going to cost about as much as they'd spend on a good used car, and that there's also a monthly fee involved. That's so much better than saying, "For less than the cost of a latte a day," and hiding the fact that you're talking about a five-year period. Now, we don't tell them what *kind* of good used car is involved. That's up to them to decide. And yes, we realize that a good used car in some people's minds might go for $500 to $1,000, and to others it might be $10,000-20,000. Certainly if you buy a used one- or two-year-old Cadillac, it's going to cost you a lot more than an old Pinto. **The point is, we're not deceiving you by saying that;** if you feel deceived, it's because you've deceived yourself. We tell you up front, "This isn't for you if you can't justify this expense," which, again, I'm betting causes more than one person to dig in their heels and say, "I'll find the money if I don't have it because, dang it, this has *got* to be that good."

Because we tell people right up front that there's a substantial investment, we're tailoring their expectations. If someone agrees to go past that point and request more information, we've already built in the expectation that they're going to spend some money. **You're being upfront with them on the cost, and it also allows you some leverage on the back-end as well.** If they choose not to participate and say that it's because of the money, we can certainly put a little pressure on them by saying, "Hey, you said it wasn't going to be a problem before... and now you're saying you don't have the money." After all, they agreed that having the money was a condition for their requesting more info.

This strategy is good, I think, for a lot of reasons, and it's honest; it's what you should do anyway. People come to expect that salespeople lie to them. I think that's a built-in resistance in society; we believe that salespeople aren't telling us the truth, ever. To some extent, we're conditioned that way by salespeople who *do* lie and who *do* stretch the truth too much, so the industry as a whole has gotten a bad rap — some of it deserved. But the more we can be sincere as direct-response marketers, and build in stories to back up what you're telling them, the more you can use that to your advantage. **Once someone believes you're telling them the truth, because they can see your sincerity or you've backed it up with evidence, then you're coming to them with a much better position.** You've broken down some of the natural sales resistance.

This isn't about lying with truth so you can lie to them later, and it's certainly not the easiest thing you can do. You see, most people believe just being honest is enough; and maybe in everyday life that's true, but in marketing it's the farthest thing from the truth there is. It will take people *years* to discover that you're honest. **You have to find clever ways to show them your honesty. That's why being brutally honest is so powerful.** It shocks them, wakes them up, makes you stand out! At my seminars, I often ask the attendees, "Can you guys handle me being perfectly honest with you?" and they all say yes. And then I say, "How about if I'm *brutally* honest with you?" I've found that people don't always like to hear how it is, so the truth may be a little painful for them. But at the same time, they end up respecting you a whole lot more in the end. That's always served me best. **I've found that most people who go away because you're being brutally honest often come back.** If they leave and stay gone, they weren't for you anyway. You want people who are going to accept your honesty, so that you can continue that dialogue.

My colleague, Internet marketing expert Alan Bechtold, was recently telling me that it in the Internet marketing world right now, he's seeing people promoting the latest flash tool, and all these tricks and gadgets that are great little embellishments to add to your business. But more and more they're moving away from talking about fundamentals. They're either forgetting them, or choosing to ignore them. **But when you latch onto these fundamentals, you've got the rock solid basis for your business.** Then you can take it where you want to go.

Your Unique Selling Position

A Unique Selling Position (USP) is simply whatever it is you do that distinguishes you from all those other people in the marketplace. Creating and implementing the right USP can be very powerful in terms of driving your business. The concept of the USP ties in the concept of honesty in many ways, I think, because, your forthrightness, your truthfulness, can be your USP.

The reason I want to point out the importance of having a USP in this chapter is because, quite simply, so many people don't. Consider all the marketers Alan Bechtold works with in the Internet marketing world, who are constantly teaming up to promote each other's products. That's great. They're joint venturing; they're making money by bringing other people's products to their lists and vice versa, which just makes everybody more money. But so many times Alan sees somebody launch a new product and provide an email that their affiliates are supposed to use to promote that product to their list, and he's on several of those lists — so he starts getting the same email used over and over again from different people selling the same product. That's not a USP. The guys who impress prospects the most are the ones who take that email and rewrite it in their own words so it has their personality in it. **It has some unique position of their own that offers different ways of looking at the product, bringing up different benefits than those listed in the original email.** They enhance it.

One of the best features of a good USP is that it's the one thing no one can ever take away from you or your business.

When you create a proper USP, you'll never be touched by competition or worried about it, even if you're sell the same product many others are also selling. If it's different enough, your USP can make people choose to buy from you rather than others. But now I'm going to come around to the ugly truth. To most people, the first USP that pops in their mind is, you guessed it, *"My prices are lower."*

I'm going to tell you right now to avoid that one at all costs, if only because it's because it's *not* a proper USP. Its biggest problem is that anyone can erode it, simply by finding a way to beat you on the price — **which means that if you constantly attempt to have the cheapest price, you won't have it for long.** It's too easy for your competitors to find a way to undercut you. And then you get into this wicked game where you end up making everything you sell a commodity item, where you're making pennies for every item you sell, when you want to make dollars.

How do you make those dollars? Through repeat sales, back-end sales, and the like. You want the maximum mark-up you can make on every sale; so instead of going for low price, **I recommend that you create a USP that justifies why people should pay you *more* than your competitors for the same thing.** Maybe it's simply that you provide a more enjoyable experience than everyone else; that is, you're more fun to work with. We live in an "experience" economy, after all. For example: unless you've been living in a cave, you're probably aware that Starbucks has convinced America that $5 a cup for coffee is fine. They've done it by doing things like using atmosphere, and through their adherence to rules like the one that says that the baristas that service the coffee can't wear cologne, because it will interfere with the aroma of the coffee. They've created an entire coffee experience in each of their stores. It's an ambience that literally convinces your mind to pay five bucks for a cup of coffee that you can get at Walgreen's for 75 cents... no problem. It's wonderful! Even their coffee bagged up in the grocery store is more costly than most of the coffee around it, because that name now signifies this Starbucks experience. I can honestly say I think they make great coffee — but I think they have a marketing system that convinces you it's even better than it is.

So keep that in mind. **Maybe you can offer better customer service, or faster delivery, or bonus materials and support that no one else offers with the same products.** Most top affiliates who sell other people's products for a living online become super-affiliates and make a fortune by adding personal coaching and instruction, or bonuses you can't get by buying the items from anybody else. "Sure, everybody else is selling the same product. But when you come to me you get this bonus worth $5,000," or whatever. I see it all the time. This works great in network marketing, by the way, where everybody is trying to sell the same thing.

So when you've got a list, that's what you want to really focus on: how you can overcome this for your customers in a very open way, so you can ballyhoo it and make it part of my marketing. **The key to creating a viable USP is to study your competition,** and this is the one thing most people have the most trouble swallowing and applying, as I indicated in the last chapter. But when they do, they without fail report that it was the smartest thing they ever did. Be your competitor's customer. Study their processes. Make a purchase. See what they did to get the purchase. See how their ordering system works. Then call them with a question, and see how their support is. All along the way, make a checklist and look for weaknesses you can verify and document, study them and how you can overcome them in your business, and play that up as your USP.

The best example of this that everybody knows is

McDonald's and Burger King. McDonald's used to make a bunch of burgers they would slap together a certain way and put out under lights, and when you pull up and go, "I don't want pickles on mine," it's, "Pull over here to the side and we'll get it to you in a minute," and you wait 15 minutes. Everything's ready to go until you want something different. Burger King studied this process, and their entire business model is, "We'll put your burger together the way *you* want it," and I think it did fairly well for them. **Weak spots like these are USP opportunities.**

Here's another example: Alan Bechtold buys things all the time from people who make it easier for him to place an order quickly. For example, he buys all his office supplies from Staples. Now, he has an Office Depot and an OfficeMax not too far from his office; but where he lives, traffic is terrible in the winter. He's been known to take two hours to make a quick office-supply run. So he orders everything online from Quill, because he noticed he'd order from them online, and the next day there would be a box in the mail with what he ordered. As long as you're planning at least 24 hours ahead, there's not much you need to leave the office for. Even out-of-season, when traffic is less congested and he can get back and forth in 20 minutes, **he will put in an order online. It's easier.**

So first, they've done a great job of making it easy to order; and second, you have the instant gratification of getting it the next morning. Now Alan can't imagine ordering from anybody else. Like most of us, he'll actually pay more for features like that — although their prices are actually pretty low. I do know he gladly pays more for his dry cleaning from a place that offers free pickup and delivery to his office. He makes a call and they come pick up his clothes — and four days later it's like Christmas, and he gets all these neat clothes that he wasn't expecting and forgot all about! It's kind of fun; what a great business model! He found out about them when they went around and stuck little cards at every office in his building saying, "Hey, we'll pick it up." That was their USP over all the other dry cleaners around, and now they're making a killing with it

So this is where you can shine: with a USP that makes it profitable for you to sell everything you sell for more than your competitors — like that dry cleaner — **and sell more of them, too.** Alan's dry cleaner story reminds me of one of the best USP stories that I personally know of, that of Enterprise Rent-a-Car, which has that same basic USP: "We'll pick you up." The founder is a multi-multi-billionaire; three out of five of his multi-billion dollar companies have made it to the Fortune 500. When he first decided to get into that business, he was hit with the fact that its two biggest competitors were Avis and Hertz. Those companies, as well as several others, all hang around the airports and pay huge amounts of money to do so. Plus, there was nothing that unique about any of them, and the Enterprise guys didn't want to play the low ball game; so they came up with a strategy that completely avoided having to go head-to-head with rental car companies that were already well established in every airport. They started looking for other gaps in the marketplace — markets that weren't being tapped, like car dealerships that didn't have loaner cars and insurance companies. They're also heavy on the customer service.

Alan Bechtold likes to tell about the time he flew into Kansas City International. He was visiting his family and coming down to a seminar down in Wichita — and it was snowing horribly. So the Enterprise lady looked at his car and said, "You're not getting anywhere in that. It's terrible outside," and she gave him a free upgrade to a SUV four-wheel drive. Do you think that makes Alan go back to Enterprise? And how about the fact that if you're stranded in any major city and your car breaks down, you call them and they take good care of you? Again, they studied the competition and beat them based on the gaps in what they were offering. Here's another example: look at Avis. With Hertz so overwhelmingly #1, they came along and said, "Hey, we can't become #1. It's going to be impossible," so they just told everyone, "We're #2, but we try harder!" They're the underdog. That was a good move on their part.

Find a good USP and stick to it. Don't undermine it by trying to compete where you can't. Recently Starbucks came out with their dollar cup of coffee, and I told my wife, "That's a major mistake." You see, they're kind of reneging on the USP that people are used to. I haven't heard anything about the promotion after that, so I hope they ended it as soon as they started it. I'm a big fan of coffee, and I know why they're doing it. They're under pressure from McDonald's, which is now serving gourmet coffee, and Dunkin' Donuts is making its stores into coffee shops. There's a series of Dunkin' Donuts commercials where people are standing in line at a coffee shop and they're all going, "I can't even pronounce that. I can't even make my mind say that. Is it French or Italian?" Their USP is, "We serve the same coffee those other guys do, but we do with it in English."

But Starbucks is the Cadillac of its class; it shouldn't deviate from their USP. And speaking of Cadillac, the car dealer's doing it, too. I was disappointed when they came out with their CTS Class. Now you can get a brand new Cadillac now for about the same cost as a high-end Chevy. When you fall into that game, that's when the downfall starts, I think. You lose your edge.

One other point about the USP: when other marketers and I discuss this with people new to the business, they act like we've put them in a round room and told them to go sit in a corner. They're so confused; they have no idea what their USP is. Well, it's not something you just find; **it's up to you to define it.** You have to create it after examining the marketplace just like Alan Bechtold's dry cleaner did. They looked around for that competitive advantage, found one, and built a USP around it. They could have tried to place more Yellow Pages ads than the other dry cleaners. They could have tried to run more specials and discount their prices; but in fact, their prices are actually slightly higher. They found something the others weren't doing, and made it easier to order.

The USP can be whatever you want it to be; that's what throws some people. To use another of Alan's examples, he went with his pest control company because they're silly. Their company vehicles look like bugs and rodents, and that makes them stand out in people's minds. Some of those people will think, "I guess I'll try these guys. They're silly. I'm silly. Maybe we'll get along." It's not that they're any better than anybody else, necessarily; **they stand out, and they chose that angle to stand out, and it's pretty cool.**

Creating your USP is pretty easy; really, all you have to do is bite the bullet and get past your aversion to buying from your competitors. **The only way you can know how you differentiate your business from your competitors is to know your competitors.** As painful as it may seem, buying from them is the best espionage work you can do — and better yet, it's 100% legal. Look at it that way and it'll make it fun! So order online or by mail, if it's an Internet or mail order company. Get on their mailing lists, and examine the offers they send you. If your competitors have brick-and-mortar stores, go visit them. If you don't want to be seen there, send some of your staff in to shop; give them twenty bucks and tell them to go buy something and see how they're treated. Check things out. Try to return something and see how they react, and how they treat you. **Along the way you'll learn what they're doing, you'll learn their offers, and you'll know what their USPs are, which is vitally important.** Now, they may not call it a USP. You may have to do a little digging, but you'll be able to find out what they're doing to differentiate themselves — if anything.

It amazes me how many people want to compromise on price, at least at first. And that *can* work. But instead of trying to be different by having a high price, they attempt to be different by having a lower price. But hey, again, if you can lower your price, so can your competitors. **In a competitive market, you can end up in a situation where the prices just continue to get lower and your profit margins continue to shrink.** There's *always* someone crazy enough to undercut your prices. If you continue to try to compete on price, all of a sudden nobody is making any money and you're all going out of business. Instead, you can have a relatively high price in your marketplace, and you can demand that because of the service you provide — because you'll pick them up, if you're a car rental company, or any number of other unique things that you can do to set yourself apart above and make yourself better than your competition. That's a good USP. You'd be surprised how much more people are willing to pay for good service.

There used to be two options for gas just about everywhere: self service and full service. Some people would be willing to pay more per gallon for a full service gas station that would wash their windows, check their oil, check their filter, and such. It was worth the extra fee to have someone else do all that for them, while they stayed out of the weather. That practice is all but gone, but the point is, **people are willing to pay more than you would think for good service, for above-and-beyond benefits.** You just have to identify what those are, and once you've done that in your industry, you'd be surprised how much of a premium price you can charge for your products and services.

Alan Bechtold used to buy his audio gear at a shop next to a K-Mart that sold, much cheaper, the same stuff. He asked the guy one day, "Man, doesn't it hurt you having K-Mart over there?" and he says, "Not a bit. I get all kinds of people over here asking me for the incredible advice that I give them." I said, "Well, doesn't it bother you if they then go back to K-Mart and buy anyway?" And he says, "No, if they don't buy here, they weren't going to pay my price anyway. But they tell their friends, and many of their friends value the fact that I also give them the after-service. It's enough, and my business is rockin'. I'm glad these people that are out looking for a bargain find me, then go over there and find out right away that K-Mart's price is no bargain, because there's no support. If they go back over there and buy after they talk to me? No big deal." **So don't be afraid of sending people away with a higher price because you offer more.**

Pain: The Strong Motivator

One of the basics of human nature is that people will do more to avoid pain than to gain pleasure, which makes this one of the strongest marketing strategies you can use. In most situations I know of, if you're waiting until the prospect is in pain, it's too late — unless your whole strategy is to run an ad in the Yellow Pages. As a matter of fact, that's the only action a Yellow Pages ad gets you if you're a local business: people already in pain. They open up that book for a last-minute solution. **But if you prepare them properly by showing them the pain that's going to come if they don't buy now, you prevent their pain.** People will avoid pain like mad, and pay you for the privilege if you do it. Focus on what's hurting in their lives or is going to hurt, or, even more to point, what's going to hurt if they choose not to buy what you're selling now.

A good example of that is a recent commercial I noticed for an auto insurance company I won't name — but you'll probably recognize it. They've announced that they've added free coverage for pets involved in auto accidents. They focus on the fact that an accident is going to happen to you one day, by showing you statistics. It's almost impossible to drive "X" number of years and not have a fender bender or something. And then they focus on how much you care about your pets, and the fact that they're loving companions who ride trustingly with you. Up until now, no one has offered comprehensive pet coverage at no additional charge in an auto insurance plan, and I know they're selling a boatload of their insurance programs with that one very clever addition. Of course, they don't go into detail how much they're going to pay you. I mean, if it's a $10,000 registered Rottweiler, are they going to give you ten grand to get another one? I don't know. Maybe they'll just pay the doctor's bills up to a certain amount. But then they make the point that you get it automatically, so it's not even an issue.

If you use this sort of tactic (and you should), focus on this: how will the prospects' lives get worse *without* what you're selling? What added pain are they going to have in their lives if they put off buying from you? **Let them know in no uncertain terms, and then twist the knife a bit by pointing out how this pain is going to affect other aspects of their lives. Next, offer the solution — your product.** Insurance really is the best example of this that I can imagine. When you think about it, any insurance is sold on the prospect of coming pain. You don't see people rushing to the hospital to sell you insurance when you're in the bed. They sell it to you to cover you in case you go there. Take life insurance: they're selling us something that we can't even collect until we're gone. And at first the reaction would be, "So what do I care? I'm gone. It doesn't matter anymore." Well, if you notice, they play up the family issue: how are you going to take care of your loved ones you're leaving behind? You don't want to strap them with your bills. You don't want to strap them with paying to bury you. So, again, they're taking advantage of the pain by illustrating people discussing it or sitting around at the funeral parlor trying to decide what coffin to buy, and then pointing out that their insurance would solve that whole problem. **Offer the solution — your product — and build on it by pointing out the pain they *will* see in their lives by not having it.**

A good example of that would be financial services. These guys constantly talk about what will happen down the road if you don't plan ahead now. They gloss over the fact that you'll have to put away money you could be having fun spending by pointing out the lifestyle you can enjoy later by doing so now. **In this case, the pain is what will happen to you if you don't prepare.**

It's up to us to make it real. We've got to make people feel that pain... and it can be difficult. Some offers are better than others for it, and some people don't use the principle at all. In some cases it may be because they find it distasteful, but in most cases I think that it's because they don't even think that far. Again, most of them take a Yellow Pages attitude. They're aiming their marketing at people who are already in pain. And that's good; you'll surely make some sales that way. **But you're missing the boat if you don't also market on the advance warning of the pain coming.**

Agitating people's pain doesn't work for every product or promotion, but it certainly can work for almost all of them to some degree, even business opportunities. I see this line used a lot very effectively: "You can keep doing what you've been doing and get the same result you're getting now..." (there's the pain) "...or you can buy my product and start doing something that's going to make a difference." So it's possible to twist almost any promotion into it. I think the reason, that a lot of people don't use it is because they're just scared. I know I have been. The longer I do this type of marketing, the more comfortable I am with that message; but for years, I was too afraid to put anything negative in my marketing. It was just fear. I didn't want to upset people by pointing to the pain. Sometimes it's like poking a guy with a sore on his arm to make him want your bandage. But it's not physical pain we're talking about here; **it's a more psychic pain, and in the end what you've got to do is realize that you're helping them prepare.** You're helping people by telling them, "This message is important enough for me to twist the knife a little so you take action."

The thing that you have to keep in mind is that if you've done your homework right, you've identified pain that they're experiencing already. **You don't have to feel bad about bringing it up, because ideally your product or service offers the solution.** If you keep that in mind, then what you're doing is sort of like when you go to the doctor and the doctor does tests on you and confirms that you're sick. The doctor isn't really doing you any harm by pointing out the obvious. You already know you're sick; that's why you went to the doctor. You've got something not working quite right. Maybe you've broken your arm or foot; the doctor points out the pain and then tells you, "Here's what I'm going to do to fix that. I'm going to put you in a brace," or "I'm going to give you this drug," or "I'm going to do this for you," or whatever the case may be. Before they can fix the problem, they test and figure out what the problem is.

Marketing is much the same. **You're not telling the prospect something they don't know.** You're just making them aware of it; showing them why the pain is there, showing them how you and your product or service can offer the solution to that pain. No one gets mad at the doctor for telling them something they already know; they go to the doctor to get fixed. **Well, you can be the "doctor" of your product or service.** You can have people coming to you because you offer the solution to their pain.

Believability

Believe it or not, **believability is more important than**

creditability — particularly in marketing. Believability can be a part of your USP, part of how you position your company, and how you position your marketing messages. You can build believability in everything you do, and it's a good idea; **it's a way of positioning yourself so you're perceived by clients as authentic.** As we move into this new era in which everybody talks to everybody on the Web and you can check out prices and compare things easily, what people want to know the most is: can they trust you? Making yourself believable and trustworthy is one of the best things you can do to make tremendous sales in this commodity-driven world. Authenticity can help build that ability to trust you.

Joe Pine and Jim Gilmore have written a great book called *Authenticity: What Consumers Really Want.* **I recommend you look it up.** It's a bit of a dense read, but it's packed with incredibly good tips. As they point out, you can be a complete and total fake if you're authentic about the way you present yourself as a fake, and *still* come across as believable! You won't see a better example of this than Las Vegas. It's right there in your face; it's been turned into a replica of other great cities around the world. Drive up and down the strip and you can visit Paris or Egypt, take a boat ride in Venice, or drop into New York City. They're all there, and none of them is the real thing, although they do a great job of building something that looks and feels authentic — enough so that you can momentarily forget it's not real, and just enjoy the experience. This is why millions of visitors to Vegas are now reporting that they prefer visiting the artificial versions to traveling to the real thing... because the fake Venice at the Venetian is "so very close to real," and the casino is even more fun. Fake fur is another great example. Today we tend to prefer fake fur to real fur, because of the concerns for animal cruelty, and there are companies that pride themselves on being premiere manufacturers of fake fur. Now, some of them use the term "faux fur." It doesn't quite sound "fake," but that's what faux means. And there are actually designer faux fur pieces that are more desirable and cost almost as much as or more than a real fur.

First, what you want to do is determine what your company's focus is. Look for what's authentic in it, and what's fake that you can't make real, and how much of each you have. **If there's something fake about what you do, poke fun at it, or pull it out for everybody to see and point out why it's better that it's fake.** Celebrate your fakeness. On another front, the earlier point I made about the Mass Control System promotion also holds true: **talk *to* your prospects, not *at* them.** Get down on their level, eye-to-eye. Point out your faults and clarify why they don't matter or why they're even a plus. You can make your faults a plus. Crazy Eddy, the world famous guy who did all that great marketing of electronics in New York City... he was insane! The guy was a nut. His ads were cheap, and he sold millions of dollars worth of electronics because he had insane prices. And I really think, according to the history of the company, that he *was* a little crazy. I could be wrong, but the point is, he played that up, and it became "real." In actuality, his prices were low because he was a commodity broker selling stuff dirt-cheap, trying to get a few bucks here and a few bucks there, and he did very well at it.

Pointing to what's fake about your promotion or your business will make it even more believable when you point to your real strengths, because you can *say* things that are real all day long, and people still don't have any reason to believe them. **But by contrast, if you've already pointed out over here that this is a little joke, or "I simply do this this way," they're going to accept the true things you tell them.** For example: "We've joked that these cookies are made by elves in the forest, but those are just cartoon characters. What's really cool is the quality of the ingredients." Now they'll say, "Oh, I'm glad you're not trying to make me think that elves made these cookies. But on the other hand, it's also believable that you use great ingredients, because you pointed that out in the same breath." This perfectly ties in with the very first secret in this chapter, which was total honesty. It's a powerful weapon; when you want to be different, you this is one you can pull out and try, because you'll win every time. The older I get, the more I understand the things I've talked about here, and the more I realize that **it's so liberating to be able to be totally honest.** When I was younger, I was so worried about what people wanted to hear that I used to expend a lot of energy on things I don't even bother with about now. These days I just say whatever the hell I want to. Some people like it; some hate it. But even those who hate it know I'm being honest with them. In the end, when you're being totally real with people, even those who are offended by your message will (hopefully) end up respecting you.

Let me reiterate: As long as you're being totally honest, and that's your intention, you just can say whatever you want to say — as long as you're really trying to help people. As long as you have those two things — you're really focused on helping them, and you're focused on telling the truth — then it's golden. It's all about sincerity. Yes, you can create a story like the Keebler elves, and you can create a spokesperson fake mascot. There are all kinds of ways to tell your story. You can have a real story or you can have a fictional story, but people have to be able to tell the difference. The main thing is to tailor your story to your customers. And of course, if you always tell the truth, then you never have to remember what you said. Being a liar is hard work.

CHAPTER THREE:

Big Time, Obscene Profits

My colleague Chris Hollinger, a great marketer in his own right, was recently listening to a radio show and he heard a phrase that we marketers absolutely hate to hear: "obscene profits." That's why I've named this chapter "Big Time, Obscene Profits" instead of just "Big Time Profits." When real entrepreneurs hear that phrase, it makes our stomachs turn. We see companies being accused of making obscene profits, but how much is obscene, exactly? When we go to school, we're taught that if we want to be successful we need to study, to learn, to be productive citizens. **But then, if we go out and actually become extremely successful, we may get labeled as making obscene profits.**

I firmly believe that just about everyone of normal intelligence in America can do well monetarily. You don't have to be a genius; **you just have to be smart enough to surround yourself with people who are smarter than you, which is my secret.** But the thing is, with some people it's not a popular to make bold statements that anybody in America can start with little or no money and make however much that they want to make. They frown on that because they don't want to give people unrealistic hopes. They think poor people will always be poor, and they're always going to need help from the government. You see, phrases like "obscene profits" derive from a class warfare mentality that stems from a belief that there are certain people who will always be rich and keep getting richer, and others who will be poor and always keep getting poorer. It's not necessarily true. Lots of people who are rich become poor, and lots of people who are poor become rich. **We live in America, where everybody really *does* have the same opportunity.** You can be what you want to be, with very few restrictions; and most of those are artificial and mental anyway. I think a lot of people have a sort of split mentality where, on the one hand, they want people to make it good... but they don't want other people to make it *too* good.

On MSN.com, they offer an MSN Money site where they post articles about business and finance. You see articles all over that site, and all over the Internet in general, about how to either how to get rich or retire with a healthy nest egg and never worry about money. You see them on the TV news as well. But you also see politicians telling you that we need to hate the super-rich, and that the CEOs of big corporations make too much money. We need to tax the rich more, because they don't need all that money anyway. **So you've got this internal struggle, where many people can't reconcile the fact that they want to make a lot of money with their general dislike of rich people.** They don't want to be seen as obscenely rich.

Well, you know what? There really is no such thing as "obscenely rich," because no matter how much money you make, someone will think you're obscenely rich. Consider the fact that the teeming billions in Africa and Asia who live on less than $1,000 a year probably think the average American salary of $30,000-40,000 is outrageously obscene. But that's an artificial differentiation; there's no line drawn where people say, "Now, it's okay if you make up to $100,000 a year, but no one really needs any more than that. So if you make anything over $100,000, you make too much." **What matters is what you do with the money** you have, not so much as how much you make.

Obscenely rich, I think, is a term that comes from this distrustful mentality of anyone who is wealthier than *you*. It's a popular catchphrase that doesn't really apply to the real world, because you can be as wealthy as you want to be. Some people live very comfortably on $100,000 a year, and other people would starve on $100,000 a year because of their lifestyle is very lavish. So while society says one thing, in reality, you've got the ability to make as little or as much money as you want.

In this chapter, I'll let you in on some secrets that will let you do just that.

Lead Generation

One of the keys of business success is learning the secret of lead generation, **which is basically anything you can do to get a prospect to raise their hand and want to know more about what you're selling.** At that point you're a guest, not a pest.

Think about some of the sales calls that you may receive. Let's say you're sitting down at your dinner table, and all of a sudden the phone rings, and it's some guy with a local life insurance or financial planning company wanting to set up an appointment to show you how his planning services can change your life forever. That's what we call a cold calling situation, and most people are annoyed by such calls. **But with a proper system in place, where you can have people calling *you* wanting more information, that reverses the whole table.** That puts you in a better selling position for your business.

But in most businesses that this strategy is directly applicable to, you don't just want people to raise their hands. **You want to qualify that prospect and make them more**

likely to become a customer. I'm going to share with you a couple of specific ways that I use to help qualify the people I hope to eventually turn into new customers: specifically, I'm going to share an online method, and I'm going to share a direct-response method.

Online, you can drive people to a website using any number of basic advertising methods: Pay-Per-Click, banner ads, direct-mail pieces, postcards, or space ads in newspapers or other publications, or opportunity magazines. Once someone is at my website, I'm going to share with them some information that's very bold, that grabs their attention; and I'm also going to have a direct call to action. **At this point, I'm going to make them jump through some hoops, and I'm going to want to start extracting information from them.** For example, one site my colleague Chris Hollinger was using recently has them watch a video. Okay, they've jumped through **Hoop 1.**

Hoop 2 is to gets them to click through to another page. There's another video there with more information. It's very graphic and designed to get their attention. For **Hoop 3,** Chris has that lead jump to a lead capture page, which collects basic contact information. But remember, at this point he wants to qualify them even more; so when that lead ultimately ends up in his email box, he has other information to go on that further qualifies them. And some of the questions that he asks them on this lead page are: How much time do you have to give to a new business venture? How much money are you looking to spend to build this business?

If you look at this situation, here's how it goes. Chris has somehow contacted the leads by various advertising methods, he's driven them to a site, and he's had them jump through a few hoops and ultimately leave him some information. Now, he has their name, their email address, and their contact information all right there; but he also has some key information that qualifies that prospect. That's the time they have to spend, the money they have to spend, and their level of interest. **In essence, they've qualified themselves at this point.** So now, when they get an email back, they're also probably going to get a phone call from Chris. **At that point they're receptive to his message;** in a sense, they're out there waving their hand back and forth, saying, "Chris, I want to know more about this." **By doing it this way he probably ends up with fewer leads, but they're far more highly qualified, which means, ultimately, that he's going to have a better chance of closing each of them.** It's not good enough just to generate a lead. He wants to generate *highly qualified* leads — people who really want the information he has to share.

You can use direct-mail the same way. You should start by looking at the product, the service, or the opportunity that you have to offer, and then spend a lot of time analyzing the people who comprise your target audience. **One of the best ways to start qualifying prospects is to have a good relationship with a list broker,** because you can go them and identify specific traits and demographics of the market you want to hit, and they'll find the right marketing list for you. For example, I can go to my list broker find a big list of people who suffer from heartburn. Then I can write a headline that goes right to their source of pain, something like, "Does thinking about retirement turn your heartburn into a raging inferno?" In other words, I'll craft something I can use to capture that specific market. Having a good relationship with a list broker can help you qualify prospects right from the beginning.

In the direct-mail piece itself, you have to present an offer that really blows their mind. As you're writing, **you need to make some very bold statements and promises in that to get their attention.** If you don't, it's just going to pass by in the heap of mail that people get every day anyway. So create those bold headlines, but back them up with meaningful, passionate, and logical arguments. Be specific enough so they ultimately want to follow your call to action, which is to send off for some more information. But still, you want to go ahead and further qualify these folks, just like you would with the online version. **And nothing qualifies people more than spending their own money.**

Many of us use what we call a five- or ten-dollar hand-raiser. This is basically a call to action, saying, "If you like what you heard here, then go ahead and send me $5, and I'll going to send you the complete packet of information." You've probably seen this format used in the past. **Again, you might not generate a ton of prospects, but those you *do* generate will be highly qualified.** They've sent you that five or ten dollars, and they get a fantastic back-end package that includes a nice, long-form sales letter that sells something much more profitable.

So with every product, service, or opportunity that you have, spend some quality time to generate a qualified lead, and you'll turn a significant percentage of those into big-time profits. **Basically, we're trying to filter and screen.** Think of it as panning for gold, where you're trying to sift through all this rock and mud so you can find those few gold nuggets. **Understanding your market is the most important thing:** the people you're trying to target, what's most important to them, the best possible benefits you can provide, and more. You have to ask yourself some tough questions in the beginning. As Abraham Lincoln was once quoted as saying, "If I had three hours to chop down a tree, I'd spend the first hour sharpening the ax." **So you really think things through in the beginning, and strategize as much as you can.** It's a process of testing and finding out what works best, and really understanding what you're trying to accomplish.

We have a $4,985 package we're trying to sell to business

owners. We'll start with the nation first and then, if we're successful, we'll broaden out to the world. There are millions of business owners out there, and not all of them are interested in the coaching programs that we're selling. **But you have to begin with the end in mind;** that's some of the best advice I can give anyone when it comes to lead generation. Our end in mind is this big package that we want to sell to these business owners. So how do we sell the largest amount of these packages? Well, one of the strategies we're using is a radical one. First, we're trying to sell them a $749 package. If that doesn't work, we'll try to sell them a $495 package — and we might even test a $295 package. **The only purpose of that smaller package is to bring us the highest qualified prospects, so we can convert 20-30 % of those people over to the $5,000 package.** And if we're able to pull it off... well, again, there are millions of business owners out there, and all we need to do is make 10,000 sales every year times $5,000 to get $50,000,000 a year. That may not happen, but it's fun to play with numbers like that, and to look at how much money you can make when things go right for you.

Most marketers start out realizing that they need to make a lot of sales. **Their fatal flaw is that they think the best way to do it is to go straight for the sale.** The thought process goes something like this: "I've got a $1,000 product. I have a mailing list of people who could be interested in my product. I've targeted the list. So what I'm going to do is mail 1,000 sales letters out to get that $1,000 sale." They feel that their best change to make a sale is to directly mail that $1,000 offer to their thousand-piece mailing list that they rented to buy their $1,000 product.

And that's absolutely the wrong way to think. Instead of trying to get all those people to buy your $1,000 offer, **why not just focus on say, the 5-10 % who are going to be the most**

likely to buy it? You do that through lead generation. Maybe you ask for five or ten bucks; maybe you ask for more. We've had offers that ask for $20 as a lead generation amount. And we even do some where it's absolutely free — there's no cost or obligation. You just raise your hand and you'll get the Special Report for free.

The point is that you do something to narrow the field, to get people to raise their hands and express interest in what you have to offer. **By doing that, you end up with a group of people much more likely to buy from you.** That's something a lot of marketers just don't figure out... ever. They never learn the strategy of extracting bigger profits from smaller numbers of people. And, of course, you want the most people to sell to as possible. Common sense tells you the more people that you have to sell to, the more money you can make. So you need the highest possible number of qualified leads.

You can actually lose money by under-qualifying. Here's what I mean. Some people are scared to ask for money to get a lead, because they're afraid they'll get too few. **But in most cases, you can actually earn more money by having a smaller group of better qualified leads.** You figure out exactly where that boiling point is by testing different prices. You should test free leads, you should test a $5 lead, maybe even just a $1 lead. That's been successful for us in the past on certain promotions. Maybe just ask them for $5, $10, or $20. As I've mentioned, we've tested offers where we've asked for $750-$795 as a lead for a $5,000 package. You always want to test, and you always want to do something to get people to raise their hand, take a small step, jump through a small hoop to get themselves qualified before you go on to attempt to make that larger sale. **If you'll qualify your leads, you'll have a much better chance of making more money *and* keeping more of the money you're making,** because you're not wasting it on dead and unresponsive leads.

I know there have been many times early in my career — and I'm sure most marketers can say the same — when I put an offer out there, generated a bunch of leads, and I thought, "Oh man, this is going to be absolutely awesome!" And then I spent so much time, energy, and money going through that whole big pile of leads — and made hardly any sales in the end. That's why *qualified* lead generation is so key here.

Make More Money by Doing Less Work

This tip flows directly from the topic I was discussing previously, lead generation, and it's absurdly simple. **To make more money with less work, you have to keep selling to the people who have purchased from you before.** I see marketers and retailers make the same mistake repeatedly — and I'm sure I did the same at the beginning. They make a new sale, and because they have all this apparatus in place to make a sale, they then move on and make another new sale... forgetting that the real riches are in consistently re-selling to your best customers.

Your existing customers are the best pre-qualified prospects you'll ever get. They're ideal for testing any new offer you have, because if your best customers don't bite, then no one will. This is what the best marketers in the world do, and of course you want to be one of those people, right? **So learn how to consistently make good, solid back-end offers to your existing customer base.** That maximizes your profits, because it's such a highly pre-qualified group. You may have heard the term "the gold is in the list," and that's especially true in our field. **Look at every sal as an opportunity to build a relationship that will lead to another sale down the road.**

Here's a great analogy, courtesy of Chris Hollinger. Every day when Chris drops his daughter off at school, he goes to a little restaurant right down the road and gets a cup of coffee and maybe some breakfast. Now, there are plenty of places he could choose from, but he chooses to go to this restaurant every time. They've built a relationship with Chris. They know what he likes, and he keeps coming back because they take good care of him and have invested time in building that relationship. Your business needs to be the same way. **You need to consistently make good, solid offers to your regulars.**

There are a few key things you should keep in mind when re-selling to your customer list, of course. Obviously, it can get to be a lot of work, because **the first key is that you have to maintain a good list.** And yeah, we've got computers, but still it takes some time to segment that list so you know what lead generation piece a particular customer responded to, what they bought, and how much did they spent. That's how you get to know who your best customers are.

Another key to re-selling customers is this: **absolutely, positively don't prejudge anything unless you know the facts.** What I mean by that is, I've seen marketers go through their list and just arbitrarily delete someone's name because they said, "Oh, they'll never buy." But ask yourself: "Why *won't* they buy?" It's a 100% guarantee that if you don't make this offer to them, they're not going to buy. Now, obviously you do go through your list and decide who you're going to make this offer to, but don't just arbitrarily prejudge anybody. **Make them the offer and let *them* decide.** Ultimately, you may be doing them a big favor by making them the offer; and I can tell you from experience that the flipside is that often it will come back to you if you *don't* make them the offer. They may be offended by you not giving them that opportunity to even see it, particularly if it's gone on and made other people a lot of money and they're missing out. Don't prejudge anybody when it comes to making those offers to your best customers. Get it out there and let *them* decide whether or not it's is right for them.

**You need to make your best customers feel special...
because they** *are* **special.** You want to give them the first chance
to see this opportunity, because it's so hot. **Do that, and you'll
make big-time profits easily.** You know, everybody thinks that
making money is a numbers game — and at some level they're
right. I just told you that if we end making 10,000 sales every
year at $4,985 a pop, we'll make about $50,000,000 a year. And
here's an example I read about Steve Jobs a while back: When
Apple released their iPhones, they sold over a million in the first
10 weeks at $600 each. Well, do the math: that's over
$600,000,000 in their first 10 weeks! Talk about your obscene
profits! By now they've exceeded the billion-dollar mark.

So yes, at some level it *is* a numbers game. But more
importantly, **it's a relationship game.** I think that the restaurant
analogy I used earlier is especially apt here, because anyone
with half a brain knows that, except for extreme examples, most
restaurants could never make it unless they have regular
customers who come again and again. **People who buy from
you repeatedly have developed a relationship with you;** that's
why if they won't go crazy over something, then you'd better
just scrap the idea — because if they're not excited by it, first-
time buyers won't be either.

**When you cultivate those relationships and keep going
back to the people who trust you and what you have to offer,
you've created your own money machine.** Too many people
don't realize that they could be selling more stuff to their
customers. I used to sit around and worry, "Oh my God, we're
making our customers too many offers. They're going to get
upset with us and they're going to go away!" But now that I've
got some experience under my belt, **the only thing I worry
about is not getting** *enough* **offers out there to our best
customers... because they really are insatiable.** Given a good,

63

solid offer that's useful to them, they'll continue to buy. And consider this: **all you need is for a small percentage of your customers to buy from you on any current offer to make the whole thing extremely profitable.** If they don't buy from you this time, then next month, when you make them another offer, some of them might buy. That's the secret we've used to make millions of dollars.

Which brings up another point: **not all of your customers buy from you every single time.** Depending on your marketplace, you might have some people buy everything you offer because they're loyal customers; they like you and trust you, and they know that you're going to provide good value. **But keep in mind that even in a very successful direct-mail campaign, you might have only 5-20% of those you mail to actually buy.** The next time, you again mail to 100% of your customers — and 5-20% of them buy that time, too. Some of the same people might buy each time, but you're likely to attract a different section of your list the second time. Just because you mail to all your customers frequently doesn't mean that all of them are buying every time; **the idea is to get them to buy consistently over time.**

And keep in mind that continuing to do business with your existing clients doesn't mean the situation is exclusive; it's not like a good marriage. Your clients also do business with your competitors, they spend money on gas, food, and groceries, and they spend money buying jeans at the department store. There's all kinds of money being spent by your clients, and they'll continue spending it. **What you want to do is make sure they're spending as much money as possible on you.** Since they *will* continue spending, no matter what, they might as well be spending money on all the related products and services that you have, or that you can develop or purchase the rights to.

Let me reiterate: **existing clients are a great source of**

revenue, and most people forget that. They spend too much time worrying about bringing in new clients, and too little thinking about what they're going to do to enhance the relationship with existing clients. That's a fatal mistake. **You should *always* spend most of your time offering more products and service to your existing clients** and, really, you should see new customer acquisition as something you just have to do for the life of your business, to keep the pool of clients from drying up. It shouldn't be what you focus most of your energy on.

And again, **don't prejudge** who will buy from you or how much they'll buy; I think a lot of people make this mistake. It could be that you've got a group of clients who've already spent a lot of money; if you've got expensive products, maybe this segment has already spent upwards of $10,000-20,000, which puts them above that magic threshold where you think, "Surely they're not going to spend any more money." Wrong; get that out of your head! **The people who have spent the most money with you in the past are the ones who are most likely to spend more money with you in the future.**

Don't prejudge people in the other direction, either. Maybe they've never bought from you before, but they continue to request information. **As long as you're qualifying people properly during your lead-generation process, don't assume someone will never buy just because they haven't so far.** Chris Lakey tried selling cars for a year and hated it. But one of the things they taught in the car business is not to pre-qualify or prejudge the people who come onto the lot looking for a car especially based on appearance. Some of the people he saw wore dirty blue jeans that looked like they hadn't washed them in... well, maybe years. They smelled funny, and they looked like there was no way they could afford to buy a car from you; and you didn't want to bother trying to sell them one, because if you went out there on the lot with them, they'd take hours of your time and you wouldn't have a deal. If you don't have a deal you don't earn commission, and that's not a good thing. **So you start to *want* to prejudge people.** However, some of those people are farmers; they've been busy in the field all day. They didn't have time to take a shower because they've been working, and as soon as they get done buying a car they're going back to the field. That's especially true where I live, because we live in and are surrounded by farming communities.

So you don't prejudge people about anything, because you never know who your customer is going to be. **Some of the most successful people in America are unassuming and look average.** You wouldn't look at them and think that they're worth millions, or that that they could afford to live in all the McMansions you see going up everywhere. They don't look like they could afford a Pinto, let alone a Cadillac. But they can. **These people quietly live very successful lives.** If you prejudge them, you've definitely cut them out of consideration, and there's no way they can become your customer.

There are all kinds of books that have been written about successful people, like *The Millionaire Next Door,* and *The Millionaire Mind*, that caution against prejudging people. Sometimes, the people who walk around wearing fancy suits, eating in fancy restaurants, are drowning in debt up to their eyeballs. But the backbone of America's successful entrepreneurial system isn't necessarily made up of folks you could pick out in a crowd and say, "That person right there is successful." Put them in a lineup and you'd probably pick the wrong people every time. They don't have fancy lifestyles, even though they could. A lot of them are just average people, just as a lot of those guys driving the fancy cars and wearing the nice suits are a paycheck away from being homeless.

A Framework for Success

Next up, I've got a framework for a successful sales organization that I want to share. **These are 10 easy things that you can do *right now* to quadruple your profits, and ruthless marketing takes into account each of these key areas.** Very briefly, they are:

1. Giving people what they want.

2. Developing products/services that appeal to a specific market.

3. Making sure those items have the largest profit margin possible.

4. Developing marketing systems that identify the right prospect and communicate the right message to them.

5. Reaching and selling to those people as fast as possible for the largest profit.

6. Re-selling to them as often as possible to squeeze the largest amount of money out of them.

7. Creating sales messages that build strong bonds with your customers.

8. Positioning yourself so that you can seem unique.

9. Creating offensive marketing strategies that allow you to control the selling process.

10. Making specific offers to your customers on an ongoing basis; that is, taking them by the hand and compelling them to come to you, instead of waiting for

them to somehow gravitate to you on their own.

I chose to provide this framework for two reasons: I believe most of the points are self-explanatory, and because I've seen too many new marketers stall out and crumble because they didn't know what to do next. **Business is a never-ending game.** If you return to and address each item on this list regularly, you'll always be improving your business and focusing on it. You're always asking yourself, "Okay, what can I make better? What can I do to position myself so that I seem more unique?" **You can use your answers to create marketing strategies that will allow you to control the selling process.**

Another reason I wanted to share this with you is that **you can use this guide as your business grows.** Maybe someday you'll need to hire employees, or maybe you have them already. If you have this framework, you can bring people into specific areas and say, "Okay, this is the part of this framework that I want you to focus on," and then show them in detail how they can do that. **This allows you to focus on what makes you the most money.**

Basically, **these ten items give you a blueprint for a super successful sales organization of any size or complexity.** It could just be a mom-and-pop operation or something with lots of infrastructure and employees, but the framework will keep you focused. Here's another quote attributed to Abraham Lincoln: "Good things come to those who wait, but only what's left over from those who hustle." I guarantee you, if you're focusing on these ten aspects of your business, you're always going to have something to do, and you're going to be hustling. It's always there for you to look at and apply to your business.

In the end, the basics of making as much money as you want are so simple. **It all boils down to developing the right kinds of products and services for the market that you're**

aggressively going after. You're continuing to look for newer and better kinds of things to offer those people, and trying to get enough people to re-buy from you often enough, at a large enough profit per transaction, to make good money. Do that, and the question is not, "Will you get rich?" It's only, "How rich will you get, and when will you get that money?" Because that's really as simple as it is. **Having a checklist like this simplifies things greatly, especially when you're just getting started.** There are so many different variables to consider, so sometimes it can be overwhelming to start thinking about all the things that you *could* do or exactly what you *should* do. Instead, just focus on a system, like this one, that you can put into place and follow religiously, no matter what business you're in or product or service you sell. It really can help take you to the next level, because you've taken things from broad general concepts to a specific ABC process that you can follow. And that's a good place to be.

Speaking of Focus...

One of the points I often make to my clients is this: "You must put as much of your time, attention, energy, passion, and skills into the specific areas that bring your business the largest profits. Focus. Identify these areas and put everything into these activities." **By focusing on those things that make you the most profit, you don't waste time on all the details.** I especially want to drive that message home for those of you that who think they have to do everything.

So how do you develop this focus? **One way is to develop relationships with various business entities that can handle the details that aren't directly related to your marketing.** If you're doing direct-mail, that would include relationships with people like printers. You need a quality printer; someone you can send a job to, and have confidence that it's going to get done to your satisfaction. If you live in any halfway decent market at all, there are business entities out there that can handle complete turnkey mailings. Having someone who can handle those details will free you up to focus on your marketing and those other things that make you the most money. Another type of relationship to develop, of course, would be with people who can handle advertising for you. **One of the cheapest and least expensive ways to start generating leads is by putting nice little space ads in publications around the country.** Identify people you can call who can place those ads quickly, so that task doesn't gobble up a lot of your time. You're developing relationships with these people and setting up systems simultaneously.

Another great relationship to develop is one with a fulfillment house. Many entrepreneurs, like my friend Chris Hollinger and his wife, work from home. Instead of concentrating on having to make sure all these packages are going daily out the way they're supposed to, they can call the guy at their fulfillment house, and boom, it's done. Again, building that kind of relationship helps you to stay focused on what makes you the most money. Even if it's just you and the kitchen table, you have to realize that at some point, you might need to hire (at least temporarily) some help to keep you out of the day-to-day grind. **Do that, delegate everything else, and it will keep that money flowing.** Now, having said that, I'll be the first to admit that I'm guilty of getting bogged down in what I term the day-to-day operations of my business. When this happens I end up working "in" my business and not "on" my business. Subsequently, my profits drop off, because I'm concentrating on the wrong things and not delegating them.

Simply being mindful of this principle will help you avoid the pitfalls of getting stuck in what I call the "minutia" of business. All that stuff that has to be done, but it's not directly connected to your marketing and making money, so it can and should be delegated. **The easiest way to do that is to set up those systems and outsource it.** Ultimately, your overhead is going to be lower than you expect. **Keep that cash flowing,** because again, no business ever went out of business by making too much money... unless of course they got shut down by the government, which can and has happened.

There are so many small businesspeople out there who are working too hard. They come home really tired every night, and the stress and the pressure and the strain are just killing them. It's making them old before their time, and it's robbing them of all of their zest and enthusiasm. And yet their businesses are struggling. Why? Because they're not focusing as they should. They're wearing all the hats in their businesses; they're trying to do everything. If you ask them very specifically what they did today to make bring in more money for their company, they really wouldn't have a good answer for you. Now, I've been one of those people myself, so I don't want to try to pretend for a second that I've got this thing nailed, because I don't. It's something you struggle with. Everybody's got to struggle with it. **But the key, again, is to stay focused on whatever's most important** — and when you can, to narrow that focus even further, to only those things that are of the utmost importance.

There are *so* many ways you can outsource the less profitable parts of your operation. Don't ever fall into the trap of trying to do it all yourself, like many business owners do! They feel like they're the best person to do whatever it is that they're trying to do, that only they can do it the best, that no one else can do it quite like they can, and no one else has as good a system as they have. So they get stuck trying to do everything — whereas there are other people who can do what they need done, and some have developed systems that allow them to do it better than anyone else.

One thing you should always control is your marketing, as long as you *understand* marketing. Now, there are certainly beginning stages when you're just trying to figure things out, when there are good reasons to let someone else help you with marketing. There are benefits to services like the Direct-Response Network when you're just getting started. **Once you have a good understanding of marketing, you shouldn't let other people do that.** But things like fulfilling your products and mailing sales letters should certainly be hired out. I've sat at home in the evening and stuffed envelopes, and it's not fun; it takes a long time, and it's tedious work. Well, there are machines at mailing houses that can do 10,000 envelopes an hour. How many can *you* do an hour when you're sitting in front of the TV? You look up and watch the show for a minute, and you get stuck.

So don't get stuck in this mindset that you have to do it all yourself. Most of it comes from control issues, and some of it comes from money issues — that is, you're worried about spending money, you get shortsighted, and you start thinking that you need to do it all yourself. And yes, it does cost a little money to outsource. **But think about how much faster you could get things done.** Let's say you have 5,000 pieces of direct-mail you want to mail out. A mailing house can get it all out the door in a day, while you might take you a week or two just to get all the envelopes printed. Then you've got to fold the letters, get them in the envelope, hand-address the envelopes, and attach the postage. This is time consuming. **You should be spending your time marketing.**

There are people that can do all kinds of other things for you, too, from designing your letterhead to putting your website online to creating your logo. Again, there are services like elance.com, which we use periodically when we need things like this done. There's all kinds of professionals trolling the site ready to do anything, from data entry work to graphic design, website creation, writing, and more. If you don't want to go the Internet route, you can go to local colleges and companies that can do all those things.

This is a point that's often overlooked. **A lot of marketers have this do-it-all mentality,** where they want to take care of everything themselves... and often that gets them in trouble, because they end up spending too much time doing things that just don't matter in the end, and just don't bring in sales.

Become a Good Storyteller

Stories sell, especially before-and-after stories. Today, many of us have short attention spans, and stories help to grab the prospect's attention. That's why you must create powerful stories that captivate your prospects and your customers. Now, **what I'm talking about here are stories about you, your company, or your products or services.** Choose your stories carefully. Not only must they *be* real, they must *sound* real. **They have to be believable, and they also have to be highly emotional.** There needs to be some drama there, some special secrets, some perceived benefit or a promise to the reader. Stories help you make the sale when nothing else will.

The best stories to use in your sales material are before-and-after testimonials. This is a powerful sales method, because the story tells about the problem, then introduces the solution, and finally shows the great life-changing benefit. **The reader puts himself or herself into the story and is sold.** So when you're writing copy, long-form sales letters in particular, and you need to add something to draw people in, use a story. Stories help you reach the constant barrage of demands for your customer's attention and capture their competition. **They cut through the clutter and help your message get through, enabling you to**

connect with your prospect. It engages them and transports their mind to the place where you can weave your message into their reality. Ultimately, they have to experience a moment of clarity where they can see themselves experiencing success.

People tell me I have a great rags-to-riches story, and I certainly use it a lot in my marketing. But stories don't necessarily have to be about you, your company, or your product, specifically. They can be fictional. They can be situational. **They can be written to make a point, or to highlight the pain that you know your prospect is suffering.** Here's an example of a story that my colleague Chris Hollinger recently used in a sales letter:

Always Rising to Meet the Challenge

Today we are faced with a myriad of potential disasters, be it terrorists, natural disasters, recession, inflation, or taxation. We face these things daily. While we must acknowledge that there are dark clouds on the horizon, it is vital that we not lose sight of our most important and endearing national trait — our sense of optimism about the future, and our conviction that we can change it for the better. By taking steps to secure your financial future with me today, we are in essence becoming an agent of social change. Providing prosperity for yourself and the ones you love is more than the American Dream. Today your success makes our country stronger. Join me and see how much success we can spread.

Now, here's some information about me that I wanted to share with you so you'll know who I am and what I'm all about. My wife Kim and I live with our daughter, Milayna, here in Wichita, Kansas. We were both born and raised in small towns here in the rolling hills of Kansas. It's here where we learned the value of shooting straight with folks, and the hardships and rewards of integrity. Five years ago we started our own business, and soon became so busy that I literally was coming home from teaching and coaching and then working until two in the morning. Obviously I could not do both, so I told my fellow teachers and my principal that I was leaving to concentrate on my new business full-time. Many of my colleagues could not believe it, because not only was I giving up a tenured position with benefits, but I had just recently recovered from a very rare form of cancer. They were literally floored when I told them of my plans.

Since then, Kim and I have created a life that allows us the freedom to raise our daughter with all the love and attention to detail that being able to set our own schedule gives. I've been honored to be a speaker at seminars around the country, from Florida to San Diego. Last year I spoke at four very special seminars. All were recorded, and the information my colleagues and I presented is yours free by joining me on my next conference call. If you had attended all four seminars, you would have paid over $19,000. Join me on my next call, and they're yours free.

And that's the end of Chris' story. **You can see how he weaved quite a few themes into one little story.** It's a good example of a story that basically goes back to those key points I discussed earlier, using all parts of his personal story, including one that a lot of people wouldn't have enough courage to use — his struggle with cancer, and his rise above it. That was one of the concerns that many of his colleagues had when he first left teaching, because he had a job with all these benefits and health insurance, and he'd just recovered from that rare form of cancer.

Things were honestly up in the air as to whether or not it was going to come back, and I guess you're always in that boat when you've been diagnosed with cancer. That was one of the things that made their jaws drop. **Not only could they not imagine stepping out and starting up a whole new business at that point in Chris' career, they couldn't see him doing it after going through that whole ordeal with cancer.** But that story resonates with people. It takes a lot of courage to do something like telling your story, and talking about some of the struggles that you've gone through.

Stories really do sell. **They help you to connect, and they help put your prospect into that sales vacuum where your message is receptive.** Therefore, if you want to jazz up your sales messages and bring in more money, weave stories into them to make them more compelling.

Earlier, I mentioned my own story. It's an important part of our marketing — telling the story about how for years, my wife Eileen and I struggled for every single penny that we made. We *knew* that there was a way to make millions of dollars. We *knew* that other people had done it. And yet, we kept trying one plan after another, and nothing was working. All of our friends and family told us how absolutely insane we were, and they begged us to quit sending for all of these plans and programs! **And yet, we continued to believe there was a way to do it, and finally we sent away for a couple of good programs. We combined them and made millions.** It sounds good, and yet it's the God's honest truth — that's exactly what happened. Our clients have heard that story for years, and it resonates, because many of them have been sending away for the same types of plans and programs. Many of them have friends and family who have begged for them just to give up on their dreams. And yet, they don't want to do that any more than Eileen and I did. **We finally found a way to make millions of dollars — and so they know**

that they can do it too! If we can do it, they can do it. Our story is our connection with the people we want to do business with. It adds all those personal dimensions, it creates the relationships and the bonds with people, and they remember it. Our story is powerful. It's emotional.

So I hope that you will have the courage to take a page out of our playbook and **just be open and be honest with people that you want to do business with.** Tell them things that are very personal about who you are, and help them want to do more business with you. **Try to blend stories around whatever you're selling.** Stories are obviously very powerful when told in the right way and used for the right purpose. In the Bible, Jesus spoke in parables to get his points across; and in fact, people have been using stories all throughout history to do the same. And while I'm not telling you to lie to your customers — never do that — in some cases, the story doesn't have to be true. You can use a fictitious story to illustrate a point, as Aesop did with his fables. It's important to distinguish between the two so that you're not coming across as misrepresenting yourself or a product; **so tell people whether you're telling a real story or a fable.**

I realize that this might be difficult for you. Too many people are afraid to share anything about themselves with their customers; they'd rather not be personal, not put themselves out there. **But people are emotional beings, and we like to hear stories; we identify with stories.** If you're writing to a prospect that you know is like you and would identify with a story about you, you should be unafraid to tell it. Spend some time writing it out, even outside of a sales letter. **Get it on paper, keep it in the file, work on it, perfect it, hone it.** Make additions or subtractions as you go and as you find the time to work on it, and you'll soon have a story that you can weave into your sales material. You can use it, too, when you do personal selling, or if you talk to people on the phone or do presentations from a stage.

People can identify with and appreciate you if you're honest in this fashion (remember the power of honesty?). Oftentimes, people try to *hide* behind their company. They want people to think that they're perfect, that they're not human. And yet, we're all human, and everybody knows that; so why hide it? Why not just tell people a little about who you are and where you came from? This is especially important to the degree that it helps you tell people why they should do business with you; it involves a little more rapport-building, which is always good.

In addition to stories about yourself, **you can tell stories about your product.** Let's say you have a great product you discovered; you can tell the story about how you went to a remote jungle in Africa and came back with this cure for this disease, how all you have to do is eat this special fruit that you discovered and all your worries are gone; those kinds of things. **You can learn great storytelling by reading catalogs.** Some catalogs, like J. Pedersen and Brookstone, have very good copywriters who do a lot of explaining about the thought processes behind the product or a story. That helps draw you in, and shows you why that product is good.

It should go without saying that how you word your story can determine its impact. You could tell the same story multiple ways; one way might be a boring, dry way, while you could say the same thing in another way so that it comes across as emotional, tugging at the heartstrings. **So take your story and learn how to write it in such a way that it draws on people's emotions, and storytelling can be a big sales tool.**

Appealing to the Prospect

In this section, I'm going to re-emphasize a truth that I think too many would-be entrepreneurs miss completely: **it's all about the *prospect*, not the product.** In a larger sense, it's all about the market. **The market is comprised of prospects with similar wants, needs, and desires, with desire being very important.** I've seen marketers fall in love with a product that was indeed needed, but not desired (and I'll be the first to admit that I've done this also). Then the marketer didn't do a very good job of creating desire for the product, and was dismayed when the market rejected their product. To avoid this, you want to really focus on and understand your market and your prospect. **You really need to know what the prospect and the market** *really* **want.** You need to know exactly who your ideal prospect is; you need to know what they love, what they fear, and what they want most. **And you** *absolutely* **need to know what in their life is causing them the most pain,** because as I've told you more than once, pain is very important when it comes to this form of marketing. Once you know these things, you need to have the intestinal fortitude to, in essence, jab a red-hot poker into the prospect's heart and twist it as hard as you can so that they can feel the worst imaginable pain (I'm speaking metaphorically here, of course, within the realm of your marketing). **And** *then* **you can craft a message that's intended to create incredible desire for your product, service, or opportunity.**

Here's a proven way to do that, using your knowledge of the prospect's wants, needs, and desires and what causes them pain: **Start by identifying the biggest selling points of your product. Then find a way to put your prospect in as much pain as possible.** You've got to make them feel it! You really stick that red-hot poker into their deepest fear and twist, and then add some rock salt and grind it in. **Once your prospect is properly painful, you give them the most logical solution to relieve their pain, heavily dosed with your main selling points.** People will do almost anything to avoid pain. This simple tidbit of information has produced billions of dollars in sales, and continues to profit savvy marketers worldwide every day.

So you use these emotional factors to first create pain, and then offer them the solution to that pain. In some ways, it's a terrible, terrible metaphor, this idea of peeling back the scab and pouring salt in there. But it goes back to the last thing we talked about, with the stories. Once you visualize this analogy, you'll never forget it — which is another purpose of telling stories, by the way. People remember stories. **And people will always do more to avoid pain than they will to gain pleasure; that's Psychology101, and, after all, marketing is just math and psychology.** So *you're* the one that has to put people in pain. *You've* got to make them see that not having what you're offering them will be potentially painful — that they're going to miss out on something very, very special — and you've got to make it real.

Given the number of competitors who are after the prospects you're after, you need to wake up and understand this, and know in your gut why people buy what they buy. That's much more important than the products themselves. When we tell people that products don't matter, **what we're really saying is that the *market* is more important, and that you've got to match the products to the marketplace.**

Sometimes — again, to illustrate the point you use a story, and in this case it's an analogy — it's salt in a wound. It burns in your mind, because everybody knows how that feels; or if you don't, you can guess. Again, we're coming at this from the premise that you have a solution to their pain. You're not just being mean and rubbing in the pain like a bully on the playground. **You're identifying their pain because you have a solution; and in order to make the solution real, you must first remind them of the degree of their pain.** It's the reminder that brings out the desire for your solution, which is what makes people want your product — because your product cleans the salt away and heals the wound.

Going back to the original point, you have a much better opportunity for profit if you stop focusing so much on the products and start focusing more on the prospects. **It doesn't matter what you sell so much as who you sell to. Your marketplace really determines what you sell.** Too many people go into business thinking otherwise; they have an idea for a product, and from that idea comes the product development. After it's is developed, they sit in their office, admiring their little work of art. Then they start thinking, "Okay, now that I've got this product, who am I going to sell it to?" They struggle, then, with trying to find a marketplace for the product they just created. **Well, you should never have to find a marketplace for your product, because you *start* with the marketplace, and then you find the product the marketplace wants.**

People will always buy what they want, and they'll always buy more of what they're already spending money on. If you can identify a group of people who are spending money on certain kinds of products and services, then you can come along and offer a newer, better, faster, more convenient product or service that fills those same wants in a better way, and you can make a profit. *It starts with the marketplace.* Never get that out of your head. Write it down. Hang in on your wall. Put it next to your bathroom mirror. Stick it someplace in your car, maybe, where you can look at it every day. The marketplace *always* comes before the product. Always, always, always. **If you'll remember that, you'll never struggle for what to sell.** You'll only struggle figuring out what the marketplace wants. Let the product follow the marketplace, and you can create a never-ending stream of products and services to offer to that marketplace once you've identified it. And once you've identified one marketplace, there's nothing to keep you from identifying others that you can tap into with other products and services.

I would look for markets that are very, very rabid. Not long ago, Chris Lakey and I were looking at a rather large market that we wanted to sell our products and services to. It turns out it was a fragmented market and, what's even more, the people in that market weren't really excited about the types of things we wanted to sell anyway. We knew that because there was such an absence of good, strong competitors. That was the one telltale sign, having done a little bit of research. **What you're looking for are places where other people are already making a ton of money!** I know it sounds like common sense, and yet so many people want to be the pioneers. They go out there and fall in love with these products, or they fall in love with a group of people they want to sell something to. They see a lack of competition, and don't even realize that it's because the market they want to sell to isn't crazy about the types of things that they offer. **You always go in the areas where other people are making a lot of money, and design your initial products and services to be very similar to what other people are selling right now.** The time to be creative, the time to be the pioneer, the time to go out there and experiment, is when you already have millions in the bank — or however else you define being financially secure. That's when you can test your other ideas and experiment with markets where there's an absence of competitors.

On TV once, I saw a little special documentary about Simon Cowell, the guy who started American Idol. Obviously, he's a music guy. One of the things they mentioned was the fact that in the mid- to late-1990s, he noticed that people all over the world were going crazy about these humongous professional wrestlers like The Rock and Stone Cold Steve Austin. He saw that people were already making a lot of money with that market, and there was a lot of interest and desire connected with these wrestlers, so he convinced them to cut their own albums. And even though the music was horrible, that was one of his first big breaks. He sold literally millions of recordings of professional wrestlers doing their best to be singers. The market was rabid for these guys; **he just gave them another product and, in turn, made millions of dollars.** And then he kept expanding and expanding, looking for other unique areas to excel in.

Simon Cowell was filling a demand that wrestling fans had; he was able to get on the other side of the cash register and understand his market at a deep level. That's part of what getting on the other side of the cash register means. Stop thinking like a consumer; start thinking like a marketer. **Start looking at what other people are doing, and ask yourself how you can do things that are similar.**

Now, that anecdote on the previous page is part of Simon Cowell's story. If you don't have your own yet, start working on it; sit down and write a little about who you are, and why people could identify — or would want to identify — with you and your story. And don't write your story as it is, necessarily; maybe you haven't achieved success yet, and at the moment your story is all about struggle. **Go ahead and write your story as if you've gone ahead and found success, because you eventually will if you keep working at it.** When you get there your story can be already written — all you need to do is work in the details.

CHAPTER FOUR:

Dispelling the Marketing Fog

❖

To start off this chapter, I want to take you back about 60 years ago, for just a moment. If you're older than 50ish, you might remember this: London, Friday, December 5, 1952. That date might not mean much to you, but it's well-remembered across the pond, because it's the date of a huge catastrophe. It was a cold winter, and on December 5, everybody was burning coal in their fireplaces to heat their homes. Due to the extreme cold, the smoke from the coal fires was trapped in the city, and it combined with the natural moisture in the air to create this huge fog. The fog set in thick. At that time, it wasn't that uncommon for there to be a fog over London, so people didn't think too much of it; but by December 7, the fog was so thick that visibility fell to just about a foot. People could literally hold their hand a foot in front of their face and not see it. They couldn't see their shoes.

Hundreds of people died the first day from respiratory distress due to the smog. Within four days, something like 4,000 people had died; the smog had choked the life out of them. They couldn't breathe, and couldn't see to go anywhere. Ambulances stopped running because of the lack of visibility. Business, theaters, concerts, and the like shut down. In the subsequent coming weeks and months, another 8,000 people or so died because of the effects of the December 1952 fog; many survivors of the actual event later developed lung conditions or pneumonia, or had complications from those, so as many 12,000 people died from this unnaturally thick fog.

Of course, that was a tragic event, and a horrible situation; but I think it offers a good analogy to marketing in many instances. **Marketers sometimes sit in this kind of fog; we feel like we have a little information, yet it's indistinct and hard to see.** We can't really see the connections, and we don't know which way is up or down. We're all confused, and without the right help — without someone grabbing us and showing us which way we're going — we're like those people in London in 1952. We just can't see more than a foot in front of our faces and we're destined to fail. **We need some help and we need someone to show us the right way.**

That's what we do with the Direct-Response Network, and that's what I'll present in this chapter. **The idea is to hopefully lift that fog, at least briefly.** If you've been sitting around feeling confused, not really sure where to turn, what to do, or which direction to go, hopefully these strategies will help lift the fog you've been experiencing, help you come out of the haze, and reveal a clear direction to start you down your road to success.

The Minnow and the Whale

Here's a fundamental truth of life: you can't catch a whale by using a minnow as bait. Now, think about that. **If you want something big to happen, as in making big sales and big profits, you've got to do big things!** Bill Glazer, a marketing expert who's a real hero of mine, puts it a bit differently: he says that most businesspeople are trying to shoot an elephant using a BB gun.

Now, here's where the fog analogy comes into play. Most

businesspeople are so deluded in their expectations, it's almost as if they're in a fog. **They simply don't realize the high level of forces working against them on a daily basis.** Some of these forces include increased competition, lower profit margins, and consumers who are more and more demanding all of the time. There used to be that phrase that went, "The customer is king." Well, these days, customers are more like dictators than kings. There's a growing skepticism in the marketplace, and that's not going away; it's only going to get worse. **People also have a tremendous amount of apathy towards most marketing messages.** They've learned how to tune them out because of the information overload problem; they feel too overwhelmed to listen to everything, and don't want to learn anything anymore.

There's hostility against advertisers. Everybody hits the "mute" button when a commercial comes on the TV, and there's a strong resistance to all sales messages. **The average consumer today is more educated than ever, and is very cynical, too.** They're on guard constantly; they don't believe a word that you say. And yet, most businesspeople are so "fogged in" that they think that all they have to do is run a few ads or a few TV spots, or drop a few postcards in the mail, and people are going to automatically rush to them. That's a real delusion.

This is one of the big reasons we teach Direct-Mail Marketing (DRM) as the most effective way of doing business, compared with the ad agency methods of advertising. As a small business especially, ad agencies push you to just put your name in the Yellow Pages so that if anybody needs you, they'll find you. Or the businessperson might think, "I'm only going to use word of mouth, and if people want me, they know where I'm at." This all comes back to the quote a mentioned earlier, which is attributed to P.T. Barnum: "You can't catch a whale by using a minnow as bait." Now, I used to fish a lot when I was younger, and I know that you always match your bait to whatever fish you're trying to catch. When you're after little fish, you need a tiny hook and little bit of worm or a piece of corn, because otherwise the fishes can't get the hook in their mouth. And there are other times when you want to try to catch huge catfish, so you use larger hooks with bigger bait. Now, maybe you first catch little fish so you can use them to catch the larger fish. Someone who didn't know better might ask you, "Why are you using such a big fish for bait? You're only going to catch a big fish." Well, duh — that's what you want to do! **You're being** *selective*. If the fish is too small you don't want it, so you do your best to arrange things so they can't take the bait. The only way to catch a whale is to use a giant hook and a substantial bait. **The point here is that you have to match the tackle and bait to whatever you're trying to catch.**

In business, you're trying to catch the best possible customers, folks who will spend the largest amount of money for the longest amount of time; so minnows are out. That also means using the right bait — if your target market has no interest in what you're offering, you're probably not going to catch their attention. And if you're using the using the wrong advertising, you're not going to catch them, either. **You have to have to present the right offer (the bait) with the right advertising in the appropriate medium (the tackle).**

The unfortunate reality with most business owners is that when they start a business, all they do is buy themselves a job — and admittedly, they're usually good at what they do. Let's say they're a dry cleaner; well, they're probably really good at cleaning clothes, and can get a stain out like nobody's business. **But it's just as likely that they have no clue how to market their business, and no interest in learning how to do so.** And so all they are is a good dry cleaner. Similarly, someone who has a local clothing store may be really good at measuring you and helping you pick out just the right suit for that special occasion, but they have no clue or interest in learning how to market their business and attract more customers. The two traits often go hand in hand, but what good is a new business that you just start without the ability to advertise and bring in new customers, and continue to resell to the customers you have?

So you have to keep alert to the marketing opportunities, and you have to keep current, because of the problems I've already mentioned: the increased competition, the lower profit margins, customer apathy, and consumers who are savvier than they used to be. The Internet has continuously crept more and more into our lives. These days you can buy a refrigerator with an Internet connection built right into them, so it will keep track of your groceries and tell you when you need to go to the store. You can go virtually anywhere the world, and handheld devices keep the Internet at your fingertips. **The Internet is making people smarter consumers because they can research on the world wide web,** find out more about the products, and find out whether they should shop with you or the competition. **They're more educated these days, and demand better service.**

Even 10 years ago, if you were going to buy a new car you had to do a lot of digging to find out what the dealer paid for it. Today it's easy to go on the Internet, pick out the car you want, and know exactly what the dealer bought that car from the factory for. **That means that as a consumer, you have the ability to go in and demand a price.** You can say, "I think that on this particular car, a good profit for you is $150," and they would say, "How do you know how much profit we're making?" You tell them, "I know that you paid this much from the factory, so I'm going to pay you *this* much, and that should leave you a profit of $150." The Internet gives you increased knowledge of the market at a low cost. **As a consumer, that's great; as a**

marketer, it puts you at a disadvantage.

Plus, again, there's a lot of doubt in the marketplace in general. **People aren't as trusting *or* as trustworthy as they used to be, so that means there's more questioning.** Apathy shoots you down; it's so easy to zap forward on your DVR or TiVo and skip the commercials altogether. Many people turn off the radio or change the channel during commercials, if they even listen to a radio anymore. Since people have grown used to just tuning out the sales message, **you've got to do something to stand up and make them pay attention.** People are overloaded with information, and they lead such busy lives these days. If they've got a family, they probably have a kid going this direction one night and a kid going another direction another night. They've got soccer practice, football practice, baseball practice, basketball practice, choir, and school programs in the evening. All these things go on, and they take up people's time. Because people are so overloaded, not only with information but with busy schedules, **you've got to cut through the clutter.**

In general, too, people are resistant to sales messages. **They don't want to be sold — but it's clear that they not only want to buy things, they *love* to buy.** If you look at the numbers, even in a bad economy, you'll see that people will still spend their money. People want to buy the things they want to buy. But they don't want to be sold, so you have to break through that reluctance and deliver a sales message that makes them want what you offer. **At the same time, you want them to feel they're making the choice to buy from you, not that they're being pressured into buying something.** They want to feel like they're making the buying decision.

That's where direct-mail comes in; it's part of this whole strategy of using the right bait to catch the right fish. With direct-mail, you can either compile or rent a mailing list of people who are interested in what you have to offer, contact them, and use the method of qualifying leads I talked about in the last chapter to deal specifically with people who you *know* are interested in your offer. **In fact, they asked you to make your pitch.** You can use direct-mail strategies through classified advertising or display advertising; even small businesses can use Yellow Page advertising effectively this way, by getting people to raise their hand and say they're interested in what you have or by getting them to call a phone number, visit a website, or whatever so that you can capture that lead, get them to give you their contact information so that you can present them with your sales message, and give them an opportunity to buy what you're selling. **If you'll do that the right way, you'll cut through that fog.**

The fog analogy is a good one for another reason: Not only are most businesspeople absolutely blind to all the changing market forces that result in more customer cynicism and sales resistance, **they also have a tendency to think people are excited about their product or service just because they are.** Nothing could be further from the truth. It's a mistake that entrepreneurs make all the time, since they love what they're selling. Well, that doesn't necessarily mean other people love it or are even interested in it. And this whole idea that things just sell themselves is one of the biggest lies I've ever heard. It may have been true 200 years ago, but it ain't true today. *Nothing sells itself.* Whenever you start hearing somebody try to pitch you on something that sells itself, they're either lying to you or they're deluded themselves — in which case you're still being lied to in an indirect way.

Now, I don't want you to think that any of this is negative, because it's not negative at all. **This is *reality*.** There are certain forces out there that are working against all of us, but that's no reason for you to put your tail between your legs and tell yourself that you can't go out there and make a lot of money. On the contrary, **there's never been a time in history for the average person, someone who has no special knowledge, no special skills, no special abilities, to go out there and make millions!** In fact, with today's technology, including Federal Express and other distribution systems, Internet technologies, modern personal computers and cellular technologies and all of the future technology that will continue to evolve, you have more power than ever before — if you choose to use it. **And you can't delude yourself; you've got to get rid of the fog.**

Here's one quick strategy we're using right now. We have a plan to go out there and dominate a much larger market than the one we've been reaching until now. Well, any fool can have a big goal. Just because you want to go out and make millions of dollars doesn't mean you're going to do it. **But it all starts with a goal, and that leads to a plan.** Here's our plan: we've got a $5,000 package, and we're willing to spend up to $4,000 just to make every $5,000 sale. Now, think about that. We're willing to make a gross profit of only $1,000 on every $5,000 package that we sell. Why? Because **#1,** it has residual income associated with it. And then, **#2,** there's a lifetime customer value that's attached to it too. That lets us be so much more aggressive with all of our marketing. We can do things that most of our competitors would be scared to death to do. We can be aggressive, we can be bold, we can go out there and spend more money. We can have a bigger presence in the marketplace. In so doing, we'll make sales that our competitors would never have made. We'll get new customers that our competitors would have never been able to reach, because we're going to be able to do so much more. **And that's been our strategy in general: to be as aggressive as possible, to be willing to spend as much money on every new sale as we can** — **because we realize that the profits are to be made from repeat purchases.** Now, it's not about trying to suck money out of people; you have to get them the first time before you can get them again and again, and every time thereafter you have to give them tremendous value, or they're going to go away. **It's about serving people in the highest way possible, about making them so happy that they're glad to buy from you repeatedly.** Having an aggressive marketing strategy lets you go out there and willingly spend more money in your new customer acquisition, and with the subsequent purchases or offers that you make to your established customer base.

Nine Mistakes to Avoid

Instead of talking about positives as I usually do, this particular strategy illuminates **dangerous errors that entrepreneurs often make.** That's because I think it's helpful, sometimes, to discuss the things that you can do wrong as well as right, so you know what to avoid. Here are the nine mistakes I see all too often, and what you have to do to keep them from grounding you:

1. **No focus.** The list of prospects is of primary importance, and you need to home in on highly qualified prospects and get to know them in the most intimate way possible.

2. **No compelling offer.** You need something to get people to take action now; otherwise, they have no reason to respond to or to buy from you.

3. **No deadline.** You've got to build urgency into your offer. The more urgency you have, the higher your response rate will be.

4. **A lack of testimonials.** You should *always* remember that what other people say about you is much more important than what you say about yourself. A lack of testimonials is a detriment to your marketing.

5. **No way to measure results**. The only thing that counts in any business is return on investment. Know your numbers. Don't get hung up on response rates, because you can't put them in the bank.

6. **No follow-up**. Most people give up way too soon; 82% of sales happen after the first follow-up. You need a plan to follow-up with your leads to try to convert them to sales.

7. **Trying to be cute and funny using non-direct-response, Madison Avenue advertising**. Don't be cute and funny. Try to make the sale.

8. **Bad copy**. Having a bad sales letter can kill your sales rate. Learn to write.

9. **Too much reliance in one medium**. You need to diversify. Advertise in more than one medium.

As I've indicated above, **what you need to do is the exact opposite of these nine mistakes.** Regarding the first one, which is lack of focus, everybody's heard the little cliché that says, "If everybody is your customer, then nobody is your customer." I think people tend to discount all clichés in general, but they're clichés for a reason, aren't they? Often, there's a lot of truth in them. So ask yourself: **who, exactly, are you trying to reach?** That's the most important thing. **The market comes first,** as we tell people again and again when they come to our marketing workshops. And when we say "market," we're simply talking about a group of people who have some strong commonality that causes them to buy the type of products and services you sell. Who are those people? Where can you reach them?

Next, what must you say to those people in order to get their attention and get their interest? **Most people just don't**

have a compelling offer; but to really tear up the sales floor, you've got to do something to get people to take action *now*. **You have to prove to them that what you have is much more valuable than the money you're asking them to give up in return.** If there's not a strong reason to take action right away, most people won't. Think about those TV infomercials where they say, "You'll get this and this and this... But wait, there's more! You'll also get this and this and this and this! And, for the first 50 people who call in now, you'll also get this and this, too!" and they just keep stacking it up. Some of those infomercials have a time clock, and that time clock starts winding down. That's something that creates a sense of urgency.

Which folds into number three on our list: no deadlines. **You have to build a deadline into your offer, and give a good reason why you're not just lying to them about it.** You don't want to lie to people; we're not talking about lying for a living here. But we *are* talking about doing things to dramatize your offer, to give people more reasons to go ahead and do what you want them to do.

Our fourth item is a **lack of testimonials,** which I've already talked about in detail in the last chapter; you've got to have clear, honest testimonials to get other people to buy. Number five — **no measurement of results.** All that matters is how much money you spend versus how much money you make. This goes back to an earlier topic, where I discussed how everybody wants to try to catch a whale by using a minnow as bait; that is, most people are trying to spend as little as they can in order to make each sale. In one sense that's smart, because you don't want to be spendthrift; on the other hand, offering up big bait does give you a competitive advantage. I mentioned the strategy that we're involved with at M.O.R.E., Inc., where we're happy to spend up to $4,000 in order to get that $5,000 sale. We're willing to be aggressive, because it's all about return on investment. **You've got to know what you're numbers are, and you can't get hung up on response rates.** People may say, "Well, I only got a half of a 1% response rate." That doesn't mean anything to us. **The only thing we care about is how much money you spend versus how much you make — and even then it sometimes takes a while to close the gap.**

Not to brag, but there was a time not too long ago when we were bringing in almost $2,000,000 a month. We had a promotion where we were spending huge sums of money just to get the initial sale — I'm talking about *huge* sums of money. **The truth is, we were going negative to get the first sale, but then we had a nice big, fat upgrade attached to the first sale — plus we had continuity revenue, too.** We were just rolling in money while that promotion lasted, and it was great. That's the general type of thinking you need to adhere to.

Number six: **no follow-up. Most marketers give up way too soon.** That would be like asking your girlfriend one time if she wants to marry you. If she says no once, what, are you just going to shut up? Not likely! You're going to keep asking her again and again until, ideally, she finally says yes. The same is true in business. And then number seven — trying to be cute and funny. There was recently a promotion in our market that a bunch of people were involved in, but those people were never likely to make any money, because they were using cartoons as part of their message. **You can't be cute. You can't be funny.**

Number eight: **bad copy. You've got to write great ad copy, or you'll absolutely kill your own ability to make money.** Now, learning to be a great copywriter is a skill that anybody can learn, and it's one of the greatest marketing skills, if not *the* greatest marketing skill, that you can acquire. All it takes is learning how to put words on paper in a way that causes people to send money to you. If you can accomplish that, it's the most amazing feeling that you'll ever experience in your life —

and it's within your reach. The importance of writing copy can't be over-emphasized, and in fact I've written whole books about it. Of all these items you should avoid, bad sales copy is the worst. **As a marketer, writing good sales copy is one of the most important things you can learn, because it sets the foundation for everything else.** Not only will you learn to write copy that's compelling, you'll learn how to handle follow-ups and other important aspects of the business. If you can write great sales copy, you'll be using DRM, which means #5 will come into play, **where you'll be able to measure your results — because you'll have specific offers that go out, and you'll know the results you got from that particular advertising.** It all starts with great sales copy, and each of the items in this list can be backed with an understanding of writing great sales copy. You should enhance your education on that front at all times. There's always more to learn, always more to study when it comes to being a great sales copywriter. **School is never out for the pro.**

Finally, number nine: **you do have to mix it up.** I love direct-mail, but we're also using space advertising as well as some major Internet marketing. **So you don't want to put all your eggs in one basket.** Think of it like a chair; you need to have at least four different legs before the chair will be really solid.

The Importance of Advertising

Remember P. T. Barnum? He's the man who said that you can't catch a whale by using a minnow as bait. I've got several books about Barnum; in my opinion, he was a great man. Recently, I was going through one of my favorite Barnum biographies and I found this quote. It's great wisdom, and there's a lot to talk about here: "In a typical year (1877), the cost of advertising and publicity for Barnum's circus came to over

$100,000." You could do a lot with $100,000 back in 1877; in today's money, that's probably equivalent to about ten million. **But that was almost one-third of his total expenses!** Think about that. Almost *one-third* of his total expenses went into advertising and publicity.

The lesson here is that you have to keep pumping your revenue back into the areas that make you the most money. Discipline yourself to do this on a consistent basis. People often tend to try to get by on the cheap with advertising; and certainly, if you only have a limited budget, you want to do it as little as possible. But even so, the smaller your budget, the bigger the percentage of that budget you want to put towards advertising. And always, **always put aside some portion of your income for advertising.** That's something we've taught for years, basically ever since we got started in the business. **You need to take a percentage of every dollar you bring in and put it into an advertising fund.** Maybe for you, that means opening a bank account called "Advertising" so you can stay disciplined. The percentage you put aside for advertising is up to you; maybe it's 10%, 20%, or 50%. The point is, be disciplined about putting that money aside. Then pull that money out once a month (or whatever schedule you determine) and advertise.

This is hard to do, because people are inclined to spend every bit of what they bring in. We live like that as a society; most people are living paycheck to paycheck, with consistent expenses, and often that's what drives people to get into business for themselves. They want a better lifestyle; they want to be able to vacation and do things for themselves. What that means is that when your business starts working and you start bringing in money, you enjoy your spoils by taking a vacation or doing whatever you've been dreaming of doing. **But don't spend it all: keep putting the advertising percentage aside in a separate account and be vigilant about it, or you'll**

suddenly be right back where you started.

You've got to feed your business, and the way you do that is with advertising, promotions, marketing, and those kinds of things. **Now again, the key is to keep pumping more of your revenue back into all of the areas that** *make you the most money.* There are all kinds of advertising options you could spend your money on. **Experiment with multiple methods, and keep the ones that work best.** If you find that advertising in a certain magazine does best for you, then you want to keep advertising in that magazine while testing others. If you've found that a certain mailing list has continued to work for you, you want to continue using that mailing list. And you should always test small. Test a lot of things and test consistently, but once you know that something is working and is making you a good profit, continue pumping more and more of your revenue back into that area. **Advertising isn't a cost: it's an investment towards future profits.**

Here's an example of what *not* to do with your profits. When M.O.R.E., Inc. first took off in 1988 and we were rolling in the money, one of my best friends at the time got around our business and fell in love with it. I had a chance to help him get started, and right out of the gate I showed him exactly what to do; and then, lo and behold, he started making thousands of dollars. He was so excited! He was going to build a company just like ours. Well, we had already been in business for a couple years, so we had some infrastructure built. Steve made his thousands, and then took that money and rented a nice fancy office and got all this computer equipment, spending all of the money that he'd made! **He lost his momentum, because then the cash flow dried up.** If he'd just stayed in the game and continued to reinvest his money into more advertising, and had then built it up and started putting some of it into infrastructure, he would have never lost his important momentum. But he did, and it didn't take him long. Within 90 days he had quit. He could have ended up making millions if he'd just practiced what I've talked about.

Every day, you have to discipline yourself to take a percentage of your money and put it back into more of the things that made it for you to begin with. Period. End of story. Ignore that reality, and you're likely to fail.

Doing the Two-Step

Two-step marketing is one of the keystones of modern marketing, and it's the place that you're really going to make your money. I don't think people can hear this enough, because even entrepreneurs tend to under-value the benefits of two-step marketing. They just want to go after the sale, and they feel that asking for it right up front is the best strategy. Instead, they need to remember that two-step marketing is the safest and most profitable way to make money. It's simple. **Step One is to attract a high-qualified prospect first.** Use a great offer. Don't try to sell them too much at first; just get your hooks into them. I talked about using the right bait earlier in the chapter; find that bait, entice them, and then set the hook. Make it easy for them to buy the first time. Sell a low-priced widget. Educate them. Make them feel that they came to you and not the other way around. Sometimes that's with a low-priced sale; sometimes that's with a free lead, where you're just asking them to raise their hand and request a report. **Step Two is actually making the profitable sale.** Now it's time to bring out the big guns. You have their attention and their interest, and you're in the position to show them how you can give them what they want the most. **It's a great strategy that's responsible for billions of dollars in sales yearly.**

Two-step marketing is nothing less than the best way to

make the largest amount of money as safely as possible. Let's say you're in a large, rabid marketplace ours, the opportunity market. Well, there's an estimated 30-50 million people who want to make more money and are willing to do something about it. But how in the world are you ever going to reach such a huge audience if you're not a Fortune 500 company? The short answer is: you're not. **The trick is to narrow it down as much as you can, by finding ways to get to the most serious prospects only.** For instance, we'll advertise in some of the moneymaking magazines, because that's where we'll catch the people who are really serious about making money — or they wouldn't be reading those magazines to begin with. We run small display ads or even small classified ads in those venues, pinpointing our marketing efforts by presenting our offers directly to the people we want to attract the most. We're getting them to come to us by offering them something of value for free or for a low cost. A very small group of people will probably take us up on our offer; they'll go to our website, call our toll-free number, send for the Special Report or program, or even buy whatever we're selling at low cost. **That's Step #1. When they do that, they end up on our mailing list.** Well, that cost us very little, didn't it? **With Step #2, we try to sell them an offer that's related to the one they bit on.** That's all there is to it. There are a lot of different themes you can use here, but they all involve separating the smaller group of qualified prospective buyers from the larger group of people who are less qualified. Once you do that, you can spend more money to reach that smaller group of people who you know are serious because they took the first action.

Two-step marketing is the backbone of what we've been doing here at M.O.R.E., Inc. for many years. It's become almost second nature to us, and yet a lot of businesses struggle with this concept, because it's easy to get caught up in thinking about the total universe size that you could mail or advertise to.

And who wouldn't think, "Well, I know that there are 5,000,000 who either want my product or who should, because it's a great product. Everybody in this marketplace should want it." And so you start thinking, "Okay, if there are 5,000,000 people in my market, how do I reach all of them with my sales message?" Of course you could get their names and addresses and mail 5,000,000 pieces of direct-mail, or you could advertise in a magazine those people read and sell your product "off the page."

You get tempted into doing that because you think, "I want to reach everybody." But let's get real; it's true that if I ask for people to just raise their hand, there's no way everybody is going to see my sales message. But that's the wrong way of thinking. The way you want to think is: **"I really only want to focus on selling to the people who are the most interested in and most likely to buy my product."** So you use your lead generation tool, Step One, to attract the right kinds of people. Let's say of those 5,000,000, there really are only about 5,000, or even 500, that are the most likely prospects to buy your end product or service. **Therefore, you focus all your energy on selling to those few.**

It would be astronomically expensive to try to advertise to 5,000,000 people all at once. But let's say, for the sake of this example, that it costs you the exact same amount of money to reach those 5,000,000 as it did to acquire 5,000 qualified leads. You're still better off spending more money to sell to those 5,000 leads than you are spending money to advertise to all 5,000,000, because you're advertising to people who have already gone through one hoop, who have already raised their hand and said they're interested. **Dollar for dollar, you're always better off spending your money advertising to people who've already qualified themselves.**

That's why when you see infomercials on TV, the strategy isn't just to sell you what they're offering on that 30-minute spot. The real strategy is to get you to raise your hand so they can pack on the benefits. They just load them up and make it seem like you'd be the stupidest person on the planet if you didn't pick up the phone right now and order, because they're going to give you all this stuff for only two easy payments of $19.95. And then when you do call, not only do they instantly upsell you on the phone, but you also get a package in the mail. And then you get another offer and, hopefully, you buy from that, and they do some more telemarketing to you. They've got another package they're trying to sell, but they know that they can't make that sale by just having you look at their 30-minute infomercial — **so they just focus on getting you to take that initial step.**

CHAPTER FIVE

Putting DRM to Work in MLM

In this chapter, I'm going to discuss some of the strategies that we use at M.O.R.E., Inc. to make money in Multi-Level Marketing (MLM) opportunities with Direct-Response Marketing (DRM) methods. **Our roots are in DRM, and we've been searching for years for a way to combine DRM with MLM so that we can have all the benefits of traditional MLM without all the headaches and hassles.** Ever since I got involved in my first network marketing opportunity way back in the 1980s, I've wanted to figure out how to avoid all the negative aspects of MLM: the face-to-face talking, dragging your friends and family members to meetings, cold calling prospects, and having the big giant pep rallies where you get everybody in a room and you try to sell all of them the opportunity at the same time.

My goal for you here is to be able to take the strategies I'll share and use them to make money in *any* MLM opportunity. It might take a little of tweaking, a bit of massaging, but you should be able to use our strategies to to automate your marketing process for just about any decent opportunity you might encounter. **If you find a hot plan with a hot product that pays a lot of money, you can earn a lot of money very quickly, just by combining MLM** with the power of sending out thousands and thousands of sales letters to do the work of a human salesperson.

My first love was MLM. Try to think back to where you were in 1982. Here's where I was: dead broke. I was working as a welder in a mobile home factory in Newton, Kansas, and I was spending my money as fast as I was making it. I'd get paid once a week, and I was broke about four days later; then I was borrowing money, and living off peanut butter and jelly and macaroni and cheese and Top Ramen. I was a single guy; I had no responsibilities, no family, and I was just living for the day. And yet, I always knew that I could do more than just be a welder. I kept thinking that there was something else out there for me. Then a friend got me hooked on some MLM company that was just starting up — and it didn't stand a snowball's chance in hell of working.

You see, they were selling VCRs, back when VCRs were brand new. Of course, those VCRs were marked up about three times more than they sell them in stores, and it was more an illegal pyramid scheme and a real MLM opportunity, though I had no idea at the time. I just thought I was going to make millions of dollars, because you get so many people signed up, who go out and get so many more people, and then they get so many more people. **I got high on the idea, almost literally intoxicated by the idea that I could make money off the efforts of other people.** It was exciting! And the way they draw those circles, where they show you that if five people go out and get five more people each... who go out and get five more people each... who go out and get five more — well, pretty soon you've got 3,000 people in your downline, and if each of those people is making you an average of $1 a day, then you can sit on your butt for the rest of your life and have $3,000 a day coming in. That got me so excited it kept me up at night.

That company lasted for less than six months.

In the next few years I joined a bunch of other companies, and never made a dime. **But I did gain from the experience: I learned the benefits of goal-setting, and I became a personal development enthusiast.** I started buying all kinds of books on success, and everything that had to do with improving yourself. The MLM concept, although I never made any substantial money in any way, shape or form, added fuel to the fire of my ambition. **It made me realize even more that it was possible for someone like me, with no special knowledge, no special skills, no abilities, no money, no education, to make it.** I was a high school dropout who had my GED. I didn't have any of those qualities that you would think that it would take for someone to make millions of dollars. And yet I was ambitious, and **I was willing to do whatever it took.**

When it comes to MLM, you'd better do your homework, because most companies are like that first company I joined: they really don't stand a chance of working. And as for the companies that *are* solid, you often have to become a salesperson to succeed; you have to learn how to be a public speaker, which I've learned how to do. But it's taken years to learn that, and I'm not saying I'm really good at it, either. Plus, you have to be a promoter, and you have to work weekends and evenings.

It's important for you to understand that there's a lot of money to be made in MLM, and that's why it's been a solid marketing system for so many years. It's great for certain people. **The problem is, it's too complicated for most of us, and a lot of times it's set up for a small number of people to be really successful, while the majority fail and drop out quickly.** People get in a situation where they find out later that they really need to be a great salesperson; they need to spend a lot of time talking to people. If you're uncomfortable with that, then you don't stand much of a chance of success.

Another problem is that most people just don't know enough people. A lot of these companies like to say, "Well, it's easy. Just find five people," and you think, "I know five people." **But do you know five people who are interested in joining a MLM company, or who want the products and services that company offers?** That gets a little more difficult, especially if you don't want to burn bridges and you don't want to annoy your friends and family with the constant pestering. I know a lot of people who have joined MLM companies and were really excited about the products and services; but when it came down to it, they could maybe sign up one or two people, and beyond that it just stopped, like hitting a brick wall. You talk to people you know, and you're excited about the opportunity and even take the rejection from a few people who slam the door in your face or hang up the phone... but you finally get one or two and then you just stop. **There's no finding anybody else who wants the opportunity.** So you've got a couple of people on your team, but that's it; and because of the compensation plan, those people didn't pay you that much money, and you get frustrated and you drop out.

That's why the problems are insurmountable for most people. **The compensation plans are built for those we refer to as heavy-hitters:** people who can bring a thousand people to an event and then sign up half the room at once. **They're not going to work for the average guy or gal, absent some system like the one I'm going to teach you here.** It's difficult to be a salesperson, and not just anybody do it. So even when you're in a good company with a good compensation plan, you'll find that it's founded on the idea of a lot of personal selling, which catches most people short, which is why they end up dropping out of the program before they have a chance to make any money.

In that case, just about the only entity that makes money is the MLM company itself. Those companies almost always do well, and they do so at the expense of their distributors or their affiliates. This is part of the dirty, dark secret of MLM; and you know, when it comes right down to it, **a lot of the companies really don't want their distributors to succeed.** They know they have to have a certain number of distributors to create more of a buzz, and a certain number that are doing well. The other 90 percent, those that come in for a few months and drop out in frustration, is where they get their real money. There's a passing parade of such people coming through on a regular basis, so the companies rarely have to pay out the large commissions that come when the compensation plan is maxed out.

So when it comes to combining DRM with MLM — or network marketing, as it's called more often nowadays — **you have to find the right company.** This is so important; I can't stress it enough. I've seen people try to do it with a wide variety of different companies, and I know now what to look for. I've personally made some serious mistakes with MLM, and I'll share those here, too. But first I want to say that even though I never made any substantial money with MLM, **I was never able to forget it.** It's sort of like catching one of these viruses that stays with you for the rest of your life. That's what MLM has always been to me, and I've never gotten over it; all I can say is that I occasionally go into remission.

As I said, my first exposure was in 1982, and even though we never made any money, the whole concept was so inspirational. I went to all of the opportunity meetings and listened to the motivational speakers, and they had this parade of distributors that were coming through town and all had those big commission checks they were waving around, and everybody was excited. Everybody was thinking that *this* was going to be the one thing to make them rich! That's so contagious, and I got hooked on it. But then I met my wife, Eileen, and by that time I'd been sending away for various moneymaking programs, and some of them were about mail-order marketing — what's commonly called DRM these days. That was something that really intrigued me. **I loved the idea of running ads and then having people from all over sending cash, checks, and money orders.** It was so exciting; and yet, I was terrified. I didn't know how to get started, I was confused, and I was just afraid to start.

But all it takes to start a DRM company is to put some ads in magazines or newspapers, or mail some postcards to good mailing lists. **It doesn't cost a lot to get started.** And yet, by the time I met Eileen in 1987, I had never used any of the mail order programs I'd order because I was too afraid to. Eileen helped me with my fear; she got excited about these mail order plans and she encouraged me to try some of them. So we tried a couple — and they worked very well for us. Then we mixed some together to create our own program that we then tested. We made it work, and it was a unique way to make money in mail order. **We started with $300 in 1988, with a one-sixth page ad that we ran in a national magazine.** To make a long story short, within our first five years we generated more than $10,000,000 in income. I don't say that to brag; I say that only to illustrate the sheer power of DRM.

Obviously, people can see the success that we've enjoyed today, many years later. But a lot of people know nothing about or forget the struggles early on; all they can see is the success today, and so they start feeling hopeless, or like they've got no ability to get where we are. **It's important for you to remember that *everybody* starts with zero when they're born.** Even if your family has money and you eventually get some of it, everybody starts with nothing. The money comes from somewhere, and you just have to go out there and make it happen. **For me, that was learning the secrets of how to sell stuff by mail to people all over the country.** We turned $300 into $10,000,000 in five years simply by putting more and more of the profits from the things that worked for us back into advertising. That's a direct-response model for success that anybody can use, no matter what they're selling.

Don't lose sight of that. **You can start with very little and run small ads to get the ball rolling, and then just continue to put a portion of your profits back into more and more ads.** I think that with most people, the temptation is to blow your money once you taste a little success. But to succeed in the long term, you can't do that; if you've got an ad that makes $10,000, don't go buy a $10,000 car. **Put half of it back into more, bigger, and better ads, into mailing more and more pieces of direct-mail, or whatever worked for you the first time.** Spend a little on yourself and have some fun, sure, but learn the secret of putting more and more profits back into your business to grow it to the point where you can say that all your debt is paid off, you're living what you would consider to be your dream, and you're having fun with your money — and you're also making more, because you're continuing to put more back into your business to keep it all going.

Although we've made millions of dollars, it's true that 20 years have gone by since we first got started. Nowadays, people are a little intimidated, sometimes, because they know we've generated more than $114 million in our first 21 years of business. They think, "Oh my God, I could never generate over a hundred million dollars!" and they start thinking we're special. **But the truth is, we're the same average people we ever were.** We've gained some knowledge and a lot of experience, which we're now sharing with other people so they can climb that ladder to success. **But there's nothing unique about us, other than the fact that we had a strong ambition, and were willing to do whatever it took.**

I believe there are a lot of people like us out there; in fact, you might be surprised at just how many rich people there are, people who make our income and net worth pale by comparison, who started out broke. And a lot of the politicians don't get it. If they do, they're lying whenever they open their mouths and start talking about the inequality between the rich and the poor. They try to create these tensions by talking about how rich people have all these advantages and poor people don't. **But the honest truth is, there's a growing number of rich people who started dirt poor, broke, with no education, no knowledge, no skills, no abilities, no nothing!**

Although we made millions of dollars and fell in love with DRM, I never forgot about my first love; and I saw a lot of people over the years trying to combine DRM with MLM. Some did a better job than others; many didn't do a good job at all, because they didn't really understand DRM. That's probably the top reason DRM has never mixed very well with MLM: MLM companies seem to think it's just mailing a few postcards and that's it. We've had experience trying to explain our DRM strategies and systems to some of these companies that use traditional MLM systems, and they just don't get it.

The problem is that a lot of MLM companies are run by people who are lifetime MLMers. Maybe they started out in MLM by being a distributor for some other company, were really good at it, and at some point decided that they should launch their own company. And maybe that company lasted several months or even a few years, and then they jumped to another company and started that one. **Classic MLM marketeering is all they know;** it's all they breathe; it's how they live. And so, to approach them with a new style of marketing, where you tell them, "Listen, you don't have to be on the phone talking to people all day long. You don't have to have meetings where you bring in hundreds of people and close people at a seminar. **You don't have to do it the way you've always done it; there's a better way"** — well, they can't make that leap because they've never thought outside of the box. They get stuck in that mindset and have a really difficult time breaking out.

We've made a lot of money using our system with some of these companies, even though they don't understand exactly what we're doing. But that makes it difficult, because they try to force you to do things one specific way; they want to restrict you to their little preconceived box. Well, we don't fit in that box. **In fact, we've had backlash because of this in the past, where we've brought in too many people too fast, and they get freaked out by it.** Because you see, when you normally work the traditional MLM system, you bring in a person here and there. They know who the big players are, and sometimes there are people who have teams they work with. You get someone who's a heavy-hitter in MLM and they'll move their herd from one company to another and say, "All right, this company is now out of the loop. We're moving over here. We're all jumping to this new opportunity, and you should come too." And so they sign up a lot of people really fast. The people in the industry know who those people are, and they're not too worried when they suddenly sign up a large group.

But then you have someone like us, an industry outsider who's not a traditional MLM practitioner, and all of a sudden we're using a marketing system that's flooding the company with new orders because of the success of the system — and it scares them a little. They get worried. They don't understand it. They wonder what you're doing, how you're marketing. And then you try to explain it to them, and it stumps them because they don't understand it at all. So sometimes you can experience some backlash when you use this system. You have to make sure they understand what you're doing. You have to make sure they understand that you're using DRM, and here's how it works, and here are the results you're receiving. **You go through a little bit**

of an education process; and hopefully, you can get them to understand what you're doing. But to a lot of them, it's just outside of their idea of what's natural, of what they're completely comfortable with and understand, given their backgrounds. It can take quite a bit of communication to break through those preconceived ideas of how you should be doing business, according to their book. It's like you're speaking one language; they're speaking another. Before we started the Direct-Response Network, we first spent a handful of years testing all different kinds of other companies and trying different DRM systems. We've been thrown out of some of them. We've had problems with the leaders in some companies and some real misunderstandings, because they really don't understand what we're doing. **So you have to be real careful about choosing the company.**

In any case, we saw a lot of people trying to combine DRM with MLM. Some of were doing a great job; others were making terrible mistakes. **We took some of the best ideas we saw other people using, combined those with our own proven methods, and started developing our own DRM systems that worked in conjunction with some of these MLM companies.** The first time we did it, within nine weeks we generated well over $200,000 in commission checks. With another company, within our first week we did $10,000, and within no time at all we were doing $100,000 a month — before we ran into problems with the management of that company and moved on.

I've got FIVE REASONS why I believe it's important for you to actually think seriously about combining the power of these two marketing methods. The FIRST REASON is this: There are a lot of people out there who are just like I was in the mid-1980s. They're excited about MLM; they love this whole idea. They have been involved in MLM companies before, they've seen the circles, and they've gone to the opportunity meetings. **And yet they absolutely, positively hate personal selling.** They'd rather sit in a dentist's chair and get teeth pulled than call up prospects or try to bother their family and friends... and that's exactly what MLM companies want you to do. Even the companies that tell you they don't want you to are lying, because it's all about personal contact.

When you create a DRM system, you have all of the best of MLM and none of the side effects. So it's a real solution for those people who have been exposed to MLM — and there are millions of those people, by the way — but who hate selling and public speaking and working evenings and weekends, so they don't accomplish much. They'll be attracted to your DRM system because it really is the best of both worlds. Our hybrid system lets you get all the benefits that make MLM such an exciting marketing method, while combining those with the sales tool of DRM to actually go out there and make the sales for you with a hands-off passive marketing system where you don't have to rely on your sales ability. **You let your sales materials do the work for you, and you can multiply your efforts.** Now, if you *like* going door-to door and talking to people, that's great. But you can only be in so many places in one day, and you can only talk to so many people. If you use DRM, you can have literally thousands of pieces of mail being delivered all around the country or all around the world, making sales for you.

Let's say your numbers work out so that you only need to make a sale from three people out of 1,000. Well, you could have 997 people reject you, tell you no, slam the door in your face (via throwing your letter in the trash), and it doesn't offend you. You don't even have to talk to them; you know that they didn't respond, but not why, and all you're concerned with is those three out of that 1,000 that said yes and decided to join your team or buy your products and services. So it's a way to get your message out to a mass market without having the personal selling involved at all. **You can reach more people in less time and do a better job of effectively presenting your marketing message to them.** That's one of the biggest advantages of being able to combine DRM with MLM: that hands-off approach. **Now, keep in mind that DRM *is* essentially a form of salesmanship, only you're letting other things do selling for you.** Whether that would be audio recordings, sales letters, websites, or teleseminars, there are other things handling all that rejection for you.

The SECOND REASON you should try combining DRM and MLM is because of what I call the "buzz" of some MLM companies. **In DRM, one of the rules we use is that you've got to always be selling something that's hot.** We always look for things that are exciting, that people really want. Those are the things that work the best for us, the things that can put millions of dollars in your pocket in no time flat. I can't think of a better buzz than some of these MLM companies offer. People get enthusiastic, and you find out that thousands of new distributors are joining. They've got some hot product or service that everybody is crazy over. They've got great testimonials. Now that the Internet has pretty much revolutionized the industry by allowing such a quick transfer of the message to the marketplace, you can literally have tens, twenties, hundreds of thousands of people signing up for an opportunity online within a short period, and a lot of that is thanks to how fast word travels around the Internet. In the old days, when something happened somewhere halfway around the world, it might take a few days for you to find out about it. Today, something happens anywhere in the world, and within a matter of minutes it's all over the world. **Today, a new company can launch, and have thousands of new distributors sign up lightning fast!** People email their friends and tell them about it, they post messages on blogs all over the Internet. In a day the buzz has spread all over the place. As the saying goes, **"Whatever is current creates currency."** There's always some "hot" company out there.

Here's the THIRD REASON you should look into combining MLM and DRM: **People love the complete aspect of a turnkey system.** It's the sign of the times that we live in. The same principle applies to all markets, not just ours. **People want things that are done for them;** they love that kind of thing these days. We're living in a society where people are suffering from information overload. They're frustrated. They're confused. They're tired. In general, our heads are crammed full of too much stuff nowadays.

Sure, there are lazy people who want you to do everything for them just because they're lazy; **but a lot of people are just confused and their lives are going a thousand different directions at once, and they don't have any time to spare for a complex process.** They already have enough problems and don't want any more. So when you bring an ordinary opportunity to those people, they don't see opportunity; all they see is just more problems. **But when you have a turnkey marketing system where everything is done automatically, people just go crazy.** Our business is giving people what they really, really want; and this is something of a trend, rather than a fad. In the future, unless you're offering to do everything for somebody, or almost everything and you're even helping with that last little bit, you're not going to draw droves of people to an opportunity.

You might have heard a certain marketing buzz term before if you're in tune to what people are doing in the Internet and direct-response industry. It's "done for you." **People want to create "done for you" marketing systems, because many, many people want to buy them.** These days, we're busier than ever. We've got more things running through our heads than ever before. Many of us have full-time jobs, and on the side we've got other activities, like taking kids to soccer, football, and baseball games, and a lot of us have church activities. We have hobbies, too, so we've got to cram those in as well. We've got bowling night. All of these things take up time, which is why, as a society, we're looking for "done for you" products and services. That means that in the business opportunity world, and the MLM world in particular, **you can really increase your business by offering turnkey systems.**

Recently I was at a marketing conference, and one of the speakers mentioned this. I thought it was very telling, and I think that his prediction probably will turn out. At Home Depot stores, they have a slogan that says, "You can do it. We can help." That's been their marketing campaign for a few years now. Traditionally, people go to a hardware store to buy something — a tool or some lumber — and at Home Depot the idea has been, "You can do it because you can come to us and buy the supplies you need to do it yourself. But we will help you." This particular marketer turned that around a little bit when he said, "I'm predicting that fairly soon they're going to change their marketing slogan to something like 'Just let us do it all for you.'" They're going to begin slowly shifting towards services where you just come in, let them know what you want done, and they'll come in and do it for you. So even places like hardware stores, which traditionally target fixer-uppers who want to do it themselves, are going to start making this shift toward a "let us do it all for you" mentality.

You're seeing this creep into our society as a whole as we get busier, and especially as the 73 million Baby Boomers get up to retirement age. As the population continues to get older, more and more of us are going to be seeking out these kinds of opportunities in all facets of our lives. **If you have a turnkey MLM or business opportunity "we do it all for you" system, your prospects are going to be more inclined to pay attention**

to you, because they're seeking out those kinds of opportunities in all areas of their lives. You're going to stand a much better chance of getting their attention if you use this strategy, but you'll especially profit by getting them to see that you have something that's truly special and unique where you won't just show them the opportunity and turn them loose to figure it all out on their own, **but that you actually have created a literally hands-off marketing system.** That can put you heads and shoulders above all of the other opportunities out there.

And incidentally, whereas Home Depot offers a slogan of "You can do it. We can help," their competitor Lowe's likes to say, "We do it for you." Well, that's a good thing, because as I always tell the Home Depot commercials, "I can't do it!" I can't even hammer a nail into a wall; I didn't grow up with those skills. I'd rather somebody else took care of that. Even Home Depot now has special departments within their stores, where they refer you to their own contractors who *can* do everything for you. So the trend is out there. It's happening. **Whenever you're putting together a system where you offer DRM materials and methods that are wrapped around the MLM opportunity, you are offering to do it all for people, and they really love that.**

Here's the FOURTH REASON I think you should mix DRM and MLM: **what I call the "advantage" of DRM.** Now remember, back in 1982 I first got excited about the whole idea of MLM — the concept that five people go out and get five, who get five, and pretty soon you've got 3,000 people in your downline and you're sitting on your rear on some tropical island in paradise. All my friends would be back home working their butts off in the middle of winter, while I had an iced tea in one hand while I enjoyed the beach. Hey, even if I was making an average of a dollar a day with each distributor, I'd never have to work anymore. My life would be just one big tropical adventure after another, baby!

Well that was the fantasy. And it's a good fantasy; I mean, everybody should have a dream, right? **But the reality never lives up to the fantasy.** If you study the lives of the richest people who are making money in MLM, they're not living on tropical islands watching the babes on the beach. That's not their reality. They're living out of a suitcase, going from one hotel to another, night after night; they're pitching people and doing all kinds of workshops and seminars and training. In other words, they're promoting their companies and working really hard. There are exceptions, of course; there are a few MLM distributors who are living the dream. But there are also people who win millions of dollars in the lottery, whereas most don't. Now, I would tell people that playing the lottery isn't a good business move; let's just put it that way. If you want to do it on the sideline for fun, go for it; I'm sure you're helping your government with increased taxes and all. But as a business strategy, I would never advise people to play the lottery or go to Las Vegas.

Look, when it comes to the advantages of DRM, it's just like the fantasy with MLM. But the fantasy is real now. **It really *is* possible with DRM to actually make millions of dollars while really not doing any extra work at all.** Your sales material is out there. If you've got a hot promotion that's really cooking and you're making money hand over fist, all you have to do is make a couple of phone calls. You've got to call your printer; you've got to call your mailing house. You've got to tell your printer, "Print up another 25,000 of those. Print up another 100,000." You've got to call your mailing house and say, "Mail out another 25,000." You've got to call your mailing list broker and say, "Get me another 25,000 names!" Boom! You're making more money, and all you've got to do is pick up the phone. That's as much work as you've got to do! **It's the reality that**

all of us who are involved in DRM have, and it's the same advantage that you're giving people now when you've got a good DRM system wrapped around a MLM company.

There are a lot of people out there getting rich with DRM. That's the bottom line. And they're not working very hard to make all of that money, either. **It's the sales materials that are doing all of the real selling for them, while they sit back and collect a percentage of all of the sales that are coming in.** That's the benefit that all direct-response marketers have. It's the same benefit you're giving people when you've got a good DRM system, because now it's your materials that are doing all the actual selling for you. It's a powerful thing, and it's real. It's proven in every way.

Here's my FIFTH AND FINAL REASON for mixing DRM and MLM: **what I call the duplicatable factor.** I alluded to it earlier. The thing about MLM that's supposed to be so special is you're supposed to have this ability for other people to duplicate your efforts; and yet, because of all the headaches and hassles of MLM, most people never last in these companies. You never really have those advantages of having a downline built under you, because these people are dropping out so fast, and there's never any long-term income. Part of that is caused by the companies themselves, but part of it's due to all the headaches you have to endure when you're making money with traditional MLM. **When you've got a good DRM system, you're taking care of those problems for all your distributors, so this really does give you the advantage of having a system that's very duplicatable.** Now, as for the system itself, my best advice is to look to what other people are doing here and right now. There are companies that have good DRM systems. Learn from them. Maybe you can get involved in one. For those of you involved in the Direct-Response Network, it's a great model for you. If you have a desire to put your own DRM system together, you should follow that. Go for it! Go for your dream!

A system like this is really very simple if you look at it in terms of a recipe. **It starts with a hot MLM company.** You're looking for one that preferably pays large commissions; that's very important. I'd stay away from any binary plans, personally, but that's just my preference. Look for a good solid MLM company that does pay out large commissions, because it gets them much more excited than making little tiny checks. **Number two, it takes the right sales material, created to get the buzz out about that product or service, to connect it together.** Number three, it does take some management. **You've got to take good care of the people who are working your system.** So there's a little infrastructure involved. **You've also got to take good care of your customers;** if you're a bigger company, then you definitely need some staff. And then, number four, **you've got to have some cohesive type of manual that puts it all together,** that brings people up to speed and makes it easy for them to get started. That's all you really need to put together your own system. It's so simple.

Now, the MLM industry is constantly changing. I've seen it go through a lot of different changes since 1982, and it will continue to change. Some of these changes are very exciting, and they can help you make a tremendous amount of money. There are a lot of interesting compensation plans nowadays, and some of them pay out excellent commissions. What we've done with the Direct-Response Network, for example, is put together our own hybrid compensation plan — but you see a lot of that these days. **So look for companies that are innovative, companies that pay out big commissions.** That's important. That's what gets people excited. People want that, and in our business, you've got to give people what they really want.

Implementation

The key to making millions of dollars using the secrets and strategies I'm outlining here is implementation: taking these secrets and strategies and actually using them. There are countless stories about people who started out broke but discovered DRM and learned all they could about it, then put it all use and turned their businesses around and made a fortune. **So become a student of DRM.** The great thing about it is that it can be like printing money on demand. You can decide how much you want to make, and then you can go out there and do it. You can make a little bit of money, or you can make a lot. The key is in using the strategies. It's all about implementation.

In this section of the chapter, **I'm going to share a handful of the most aggressive DRM strategies out there.** These are strategies that M.O.R.E., Inc., and other successful direct-response companies are using every day. You can use them to make money, too.

Here's a good example: **Overwhelm people with follow-up offers until they buy.** Now, if you've been a client of the Direct-Response Network or M.O.R.E., Inc., you know that when you send away for information from us and don't buy right away, we will send you many, many different follow-up offers. Let's say you sign up for one of our seminars, but don't automatically go ahead and take advantage of the invitation we send you. We'll send you as many as 20 more different postcards, letters, and other reminders to invite you to attend more of our events. A lot of marketers make a big mistake by *not* doing that, a fact that I find shocking. **In fact, I'd say that as many as 70% of the marketers we know of don't even send you one reminder.** You send away for something that they offer, and if you don't buy it from them, you're probably never going to hear from them again. Out of the 30% who do some follow-up, probably as many as

90% will send three or fewer follow-ups.

In this day and age, when you have so many competitors and all are trying to attract the same types of people, **the one who's the most aggressive is going to be the one that gets the business.** You've got to stay after people. You've got to continue to remind them about your offer. If I had a $1,000 right now for every one of my clients who came up to me at a seminar and said, "T. J., thank you for not giving up on me," God knows I would at least have six figures; there's no question about that. Assuming that you have something that really is of value, something that can help people and make a difference in their lives, you're doing them a disservice if you don't do everything possible to get them to take advantage of your offers.

As I've mentioned, in a previous life, Chris Lakey sold cars. One of the things they always teach you to do in the car business is that when you have someone who comes onto the lot but walks away without a deal, you get their contact information, and follow up with them later. The purpose of following up like that is you know that, generally speaking, it's very unlikely that someone will walk onto the lot and walk out with a car the first visit. People like to shop around, drive a lot of different cars, and talk to a lot of different dealerships first. **The way you get them to buy from you is to follow up with them.** You might drop them a letter in the mail, or pick up the phone and call them. The purpose is to make sure that when they're ready to buy, they'll buy from you instead of from one of your competitors.

To some degree, it's the same thing with a DRM offer. In this case, they respond to an offer that you've sent them. Maybe they went to a website and filled out a form, or maybe they responded to one of your direct-mail invitations. **In any case, they raised their hands and said they were interested.** At that point, you want to follow up and communicate with them over and over — and ideally, in a multitude of ways. **You want to remind them of your offer, and encourage them that now is the time to take action on it.**

Again, the idea here is to overwhelm them with follow-up offers until they buy. Most marketers give up too quickly on a customer. **If someone has expressed interest, then they've agreed that they want more information from you.** You have every right — and, in fact, an obligation — to encourage them to do business with you, because people are somewhat apathetic, and as I've said, they're also very busy. **There's a good chance that if you don't follow up, you're missing out on business,** simply because people forgot to send your order form in. It happens. You get home, you open your mail, life hits you, you've got something going on, and even though you really wanted to respond to that offer, something took your mind off what you were trying to do, and pretty soon it got pushed under some papers and accidentally thrown in the trash.

By sending a follow-up message, you remind them that they still haven't responded. And if you're so inclined, maybe you give them a phone call and say, "Hey, we sent you some material. I hadn't heard from you yet. We have a few days until the deadline, and we have a few positions left, so we just wanted to call and see if there were any questions we could answer for you." Or maybe you send them a fax, an email, or a postcard; maybe it's a full sales letter. In any case, you're following up with people to remind them that they still haven't bought from you, and to encourage them to do so.

A question I get asked a lot when we're teaching this strategy is, "When is it too much? At what point have you mailed too many follow-up offers?" **The answer to that is: whenever it becomes unprofitable to continue following up.** Let's say that after three offers, the response rate has dropped off enough that it costs you more to send that fourth package than you get back in revenue. Or maybe it's after six, or eight, or twelve, or even 20 mailings. So it varies based on the promotion; but in every case, you should continue mailing your follow-up offers and communicating with your clients until it becomes unprofitable to keep doing so. **That's where throwing in several different methods of following up can also be effective.** Let's say you've got a goal to mail two follow-up packages a week. Well, maybe one of those is a postcard and one is a sales letter. But maybe *also* that week you're going to send them an email and remind them that way. Or maybe you're going to send them a fax.

You can set the schedule, and you can do as many different things as you can. We've had offers where as many as 20 follow-ups have gone out. We have some offers where as few as three or four go out. **It totally depends on the promotion and the amount of profit that you make with each transaction.** Only you can determine what that cut-off point is, and you determine it by looking at the numbers. And there's no reason not to continue mailing if it's still profitable; if your goal is to make profit with a promotion, why would you stop while it keeps making a profit for you?

The answer to that, again, is that most people give up too easy. They think, "Well, I mailed them something and I got this response and that's it," and then they stop and analyze whether it worked or not. Even people that do multiple follow-ups often stop after someone fails to respond after two or three requests, making the false assumption that the person isn't interested in what they're offering. **And it *is* a false assumption.** Nothing could be further from the truth in many cases. People are just busy; they've got a lot of different offers that they're looking at. That's why you've got to stay on top of them and remind them over and over again. **Sometimes they need more information. Sometimes they just need a little more pressure.**

Now, what do I mean by pressure? That's simple. Let's say you're doing a seminar, and you've got a cut-off date; the seminar is going to be held in six weeks, so for five weeks before the seminar you're sending people two different postcards or direct-mail packages a week. That's ten you're sending! As the date approaches for the seminar, the pressure becomes greater and greater, finally it becomes too much and people just say, "Oh my God, I'd better go ahead and do this before it's too late!"

If I had to define the best salespeople in the world and could only use a few words, one of those words would be "relentless." **The best salespeople in the world don't give up!** They stay after it. They're like bulldogs. My best example is my stepson, Chris. About nine months before he got married, he told me, "T.J., you *are* going to wear a tuxedo to my wedding, aren't you?" And I said, "Chris, I will never ever, *ever* wear a tuxedo. The day I die, you can put a tuxedo on me and throw me in the coffin; that's fine. I'll be dead. I don't care. But other than that, I'll never wear a tuxedo as long as I'm alive." And he didn't argue with me. But for eight months he stayed after me. He said, "Okay, T.J., but I'm not giving up on you. I'm just going to keep telling you that you're going to wear a tuxedo to my wedding," and I said, "No way. There's no way I'm going to do it."

But he pressured me and he pressured me, and then he pressured me some more! He made my life a living hell for eight months! He was bound and determined that I was going to wear a tuxedo to his wedding, and I was bound and determined that I was going to go the rest of my life without *ever* putting on a tuxedo — I hate dressing up. He kept coming at me from all kinds of angles with all kinds of arguments, 99% of which I don't even remember. But finally he got a crack in my armor and sort of pinned me into a corner, and to make a long story short, I wore a tuxedo to his wedding, and I'm glad I did. I would have been the only male family member there dressed in a T-shirt and blue jeans. It wouldn't have been a good thing. In the end I broke down because he broke me down.

So it's all about persistence. When we tell people about what DRM really is, once you really get that down and really understand it, good salespeople they don't give up. When they find a good prospect, they just stay on them. **Marketers who don't do that end up literally leaving money on the table,** which of course is good news for you if they're your competitors. You can pick up those millions they're leaving on the table.

Don't make their mistake. You're losing money by not having an aggressive follow-up campaign.

CHAPTER SIX:

Relentless, Aggressive Marketing

At the end of Chapter 5, I talked about how you have to be seriously aggressive when using DRM if you want to make real money, and I want to expand on that concept here. **The concept of aggressive marketing shouldn't be limited to DRM; it should permeate all aspects of your business.** When you own a marketing business (or any business, really), you simply can't afford to be a shrinking violet. Sure, we've all heard about reckless entrepreneurs who ended up burning their company to the ground. But I guarantee, for every entrepreneur like that, there are at least 100,000 others who aren't nearly as aggressive and focused as they should be — and it's costing them a ton of money that could and should be theirs.

I thought this strategy was important to discuss because a lot of people are afraid to take risks in their businesses, and so they end up being timid marketers. These people are costing their companies dearly because they're not nearly as aggressive and focused as they should be. **Instead, they spend their time doing all the things that don't directly bring in money, or they just aren't aggressive marketers.** They haven't learned DRM strategies; they're just floating by. Maybe they've got a Yellow Page ad running, but they're not aggressive and they're not focused.

I don't want to offend anybody here, but there are people in this world who are Wal-Mart haters. My Dad was; like a lot of folks, he thought that Wal-Mart had destroyed small-town America. I used to tell him, "Dad, nothing is further from the truth. Wal-Mart didn't destroy small-town America. Wal-Mart is a sign of the times." But he hated everything it stood for, and it wasn't until the last years of his life that he would even step into one. And get this: he even had some of his friends go into the local Wal-Mart to buy his prescriptions, because he could get them for lower prices — but he wouldn't step foot inside.

Well, I'm a great fan of the late Sam Walton, Wal-Mart's founder. I told my dad how Walton started out as a small-town Main Street merchant; in fact, he had a Ben Franklin store in a little town in Arkansas. And he was very attentive to his customers' needs; he saw that discounters were coming into the big city and making a fortune by selling products for so much cheaper than the rest of the stores were able to sell them for. So he started buying from some of these discounters, and some of the wholesalers who sold to them, just to stock his small store. Eventually he lost his little Ben Franklin store, so he took the idea that the discounters in the big cities were using and started going into all these smaller towns. **He did a great job giving them what they really wanted — the best prices on as many different items as he could possibly get for them.**

By going where the other discounters failed to go, in less than two decades he was able to build a tremendous foundation. By the mid-1980s, when he took his company public, he had started moving into the same big cities as the other discounters. He finally dominated; **Wal-Mart became the world's largest retail organization, and made Sam a billionaire.** He was the world's richest man by the time he died, and then his fortune got divided between his four children and his wife, and became diluted somewhat.

In Sam's book *Made In America*, the last chapter was specifically devoted to competing against Wal-Mart. You see, nothing made Sam Walton angrier than all the people like my dear, sweet father (God rest his soul), who talked about how Wal-Mart had destroyed Main Street America, so he devoted a whole chapter to responding to that. He was still a Main Street merchant in his heart; **he understood what people really wanted.** This chapter showed people how they could compete successfully with Wal-Mart. He basically said, "Look, all Wal-Mart can do is give people great prices and great selection. That's all. **But people want so much more than that,**" and he listed a wide range of ways that you can successfully go after Wal-Mart and compete with them.

So many of the people who closed their Main Street shops in the face of Wal-Mart competition were already weak. They had a good thing going for a long time before any real competition came along; but when it did, they almost immediately put out their "For Sale" or "Going Out Of Business" signs. They decided that they just couldn't handle it anymore, and used it as an excuse to quit. Here's a perfect example: Near our headquarters in Goessel, Kansas, there's a little town called Hillsboro. Well, they had a local Ben Franklin store there for a number of years, and then a discount chain called Alco came in. It's like a miniature Wal-Mart — it's about a tenth of the size of a Superstore, and yet it's got pretty good prices and a pretty good selection. Nine months before that Alco store came into Hillsboro, the owner of that Ben Franklin store, who had been there for 30 or 40 years, put a "Going Out Of Business" sign on his storefront. And I said, "Mike, what are you doing? Alco isn't even going to go here for another nine months!" and he just said, "Look, I can't compete with Alco." I tried to argue with him, and I talked till I was blue in the face, but I just couldn't get Mike to see it. He just kept going, "I can't compete with Alco." That's all he would say.

And here's the point. **There are so many small businesspeople who focus far too much on the competition, when instead they should focus on the market itself.** They just won't compete. Are they lazy? Are they fearful? Why, yes, they are. Are they not focused nearly enough on their customers and how to provide more and better services to their customers? Absolutely, positively, yes, they are. **All you have to do is be just a little more aggressive.** But some people are afraid of being aggressive, because they think it's going to lead to bankruptcy. Again, as I mentioned at the beginning of the chapter, they've heard the stories about aggressive marketers who have wildly done this, that, and the other thing and have blown up their companies because they've been reckless, they've spent too much money, they've put their companies deeply into debt, and they've used leverage too much — and now they've out of business. But as I said earlier, for every one of those crazy entrepreneurs, there are 100,000 others who are never aggressive enough.

At M.O.R.E., Inc., we offer programs called *Ruthless Marketing* and *Ruthless Marketing Attack*. Now, those names are a little deceptive, because what we mean by "ruthless" is simply "aggressive." Ruthless is a more marketable title; it sounds a little better in print. Really, **it's just about being aggressive, being assertive, focusing on your customers.** How often do we sit around worrying about our competition? Well, we think about our competitors only insomuch as we try to copy their good ideas. We're aware of our competition, but it's not a focus of worry. We're not scared of our competition. **We're not worried about them taking a market share.** There's enough room in our market for our company and a hundred others like us. And the truth is, we feel confident in our game plan. We feel confident in our strategy and our marketing ability. They can bring it all they want, and we'll bring it too!

I've put a lot of thought into what separates the competitors in any given marketplace. What makes one business thrive, whereas others fail? **In most cases, I think, it's attributable to aggressive marketing.** In America, where we've got the freedom to succeed or fail with as little government intervention as possible, you can't get too upset when you see people failing; and you can't be too upset when you see people succeeding, either. If you're jealous of people who succeed... well, just join them, because there's no reason you can't do what they did.

Take Microsoft. Microsoft was founded by a computer nerd. There's no reason *you* couldn't have been that computer nerd. And a lot of young computer nerds are starting other companies that are hugely successful these days, so it's not just Microsoft. And there are people like Jeff Bezos, who started a little book company called Amazon out of his garage. He just decided to have a bookstore, he opened it up, and then he used aggressive marketing to build it. Now, he wasn't necessarily a direct-response marketer, but he was an *aggressive* marketer. He went out there with a plan, and went all out to make sure it succeeded. The founders of Google and eBay have similar stories. In fact, there are countless stories of entrepreneurs who were either small-time tech geeks or even just ordinary, uneducated people who had a dream for a product or knew of a marketplace that needed filling — and they set out to dominate that marketplace. **In most cases, the only thing that separated those who succeeded from those who didn't was aggressive marketing strategies, and the willingness to putting their plans into practice, to work as hard as they could, and to be as determined as possible to see through to success.**

There's no reason that anybody and everybody who wants that success for themselves can't have it. They just have to use the kinds of strategies that we're teaching here, be aggressive, and chase it down. **It's there for anybody who wants it!** If one person can make millions of dollars, then *you* can make millions of dollars, too. Is it going to be easy for you? Probably not, but it does get easier as you go along.

Practice Makes Perfect

Now, let's take a closer look at that last statement in the previous section. As hard as succeeding in marketing may be, **it really *does* get easier as you go along;** all of the hard stuff becomes routine after you do it a thousand times. That's not meant to be cute: it's the absolute truth. And yet so many people never get it. **They give up way too soon, so they never develop the necessary knowledge, skills and experience to succeed.**

There was a great entrepreneur named Joe Carbo died in the early 1980s, and he used to say, **"Everything is difficult until it becomes easy."** I thought he was such a genius for saying that, and then I found that an ancient philosopher had said the same about 2,000 years ago. Ideas are transferable; the same methods that work for one person can work for all, as long as you've put in the time and gained the experience you need. It's like a cake recipe, if you really think about it. I'm a terrible cook; I can cook about seven different things and that's about it, and I don't do a good job cooking any of them. But if I could sit down with a recipe, and if I had the patience to follow it and do the work that's necessary to do exactly what it says to do, I can make something that tastes pretty good. Will it taste as good as the person who invented it or a great chef could make it? No. But if the recipe's written right and I follow it to the letter, I can make something that's tasty.

The same thing is true with making money. When you look at the people out there who are making millions of dollars, the biggest mistake you can make is to think that somehow, someway, those people are better than you. They're not. They've developed certain knowledge and skills, that's all. They've got the experience. Sometimes they have a little bravado. **They have a lot of genuine confidence, because they've actually paid the price: they've learned the things that have to be learned.** Now they've got the skills that allow them to make it look easy — and all of a sudden you start thinking, "My God, I could never do that." And yet, you fail to appreciate the fact that it took them years to develop those skills. They learned just like you have to: they started from the beginning.

Now, of course there are shortcuts. **That's what our Direct-Response Network is supposed to be: a shortcut.** If people use the services we provide in the three business and coaching programs we've put together, they can learn how to apply the same marketing strategies that have made us so much money, except much faster. But it still takes some practice, and the more money you want to make, the more you have to practice.

So again, remember that as hard as something may be, it gets easier. So don't give up before you reach that point. I went to a basketball game recently, and at halftime they carted out some guy they plucked from the stands for a contest. He had three baskets to make. One was from the free throw line, and if he made that basket he'd get a little bit of money. Then they brought him back to the three-point line and he had to make a three-point basket, and if he did that, he made a little bit more money. And then they backed him all the way up to half court, and if he could make that half court shot, just one throw, he got the big prize — something like $100,000.

Now, obviously it's a little easier to shoot the free throw than the three-point shot, and it's a little easier to shoot the three-point shot than it is to shoot the half-court shot. But if he stood there all day practicing making free throws, whenever it came time for him to shoot the one that was worth the money, he'd have a better ability to do so. The same goes for the three-point shot. And the half-court shot, even though it's a little more luck than skill, if you were to sit there all day long and practice half-court shots, you'd get better, and you might make them. Even though it's rare, your frequency of making that kind of shot would get a lot better, because you practiced over and over again.

By plucking somebody out of the crowd, chances are pretty good they're going to get someone who never practices shooting free throws, so they know there's a much higher chance that person will miss. If they were to grab someone from one of the two basketball teams and put them at the free throw line and say, "All right, you're going to win money if you make a free throw," well, they're a lot more likely to make that free throw. A pretty good player — either at the college level or professional level — should make a free throw about three times out of four without much of a problem.

So there's a big difference between someone who practices and plays the game, and someone who just gets out there once. *Everything* **in life gets easier when you do it over and over. That's certainly true of marketing, and of DRM specifically.** You don't have to do it a thousand times before it becomes easy, but it *will* become easier the more you do it. So writing that first sales letter can be the hardest thing you do, but by the time you've written ten of them, it gets a little easier. And certainly by the time you've written your thousandth sales letter, it becomes much easier. That doesn't mean it doesn't take a lot of time, and there's not a lot of strategy and planning involved, but you can get all that organized and done with a fraction of the initial worry and difficulty.

Here's a related principle that's attributed to George Washington: "It's wonderful how much we can do if we're always doing." I think that ties in well with this strategy, **because if you're always doing, that means you're getting better.** And we like to say that there's no such thing as making mistakes; there are just certain outcomes with marketing, where maybe things didn't come out as you hoped they would. Well, you learn from that and you move on. **Keep doing, and the more you'll get used to the things you need to do to succeed.** The more you'll get comfortable with them, and the better you'll become at them; because you'll start learning what you didn't do right, what didn't get you the results you were looking for. You'll start learning systems. You'll start developing good habits that can help you get what you're looking for and achieve the results you're looking for. **Eventually, it all becomes second nature for you.**

We 're always having people coming to us to see what we're doing. We're an open book. We tell people everything; we don't hold things back. We've always been that way. We share our secrets freely and we hope that other people will share theirs with us, too. So often they say to us, "Man, there's no way I could do that." Or, "That would be way too scary for me." They think we're taking huge risks because we do some pretty aggressive marketing. **Well, sometimes we *do* take big risks, but for the most part all the marketing we do is backed by a series of smaller and less aggressive tests.** We test something over a long period before we really start throwing a lot of money at it.

When they're just starting out, people are scared. And they should be, on some level. Fear can help you; it's a good thing. But it can be a bad thing when it comes to trying a lot of new things, and it can keep you from playing full out. I love this one quote of Dr. Phil's: "You can't play the game with sweaty palms." **But fear holds so many people back, and they never push through those fears.**

One of the things I enjoy doing most is speaking in public. But there was a time when I was so afraid of public speaking that I got physically sick before I had to get up there and speak. That's how fearful I was! And yet, I enjoyed watching people speak in public, and I always wanted to be out in front sharing my ideas. I loved the passion of a good public speaker, and how they put it all out there and influenced people, getting them all excited and fired up. It was something that I wanted to do so badly. But it took many years of getting up in front of a group and being terrified... and I do mean terrified! — before I got used to it. Even while I was up there speaking, I was shaking in my boots! I lost my voice on more than one occasion. Some of my public speaking early on was just terrible.

And yet, I just kept at it and at it and at it. I'm not going to tell you that I'm a good public speaker now, because I don't think I am. Yet I hold my own, and it's something I really enjoy now. **You see, I really wanted to do it... and yet I was afraid to at first.** And yes, I was afraid for a number of years while I was doing it. And yet I did it over and over and over, year after year... until now, it's one of the things I enjoy most in this world.

The first sales letter that I ever wrote that made our company any substantial amount of money was for a product called "The $2,500 Weekend." **We did over a million dollars with this one sales letter, and I spent three months of my life working on it.** I spent a significant portion of every single day working on it. Today, I could write that same sales letter in a week or less. If Chris Lakey was helping me, I could write it in two days. So things *do* get easier.

A while back I did a call with a friend of ours in Canada, a Direct-Response Network member. He asked me, "How do you come up with all your multi-million dollar ideas?" Well, I didn't have an answer for him, except to say that we've been in the same market since 1988. **We really have a good handle on what our clients want.** We've had a lot of successful promotions. We've learned what they *don't* want, we've got the experience behind us, and it makes it easy for us to do it. Is it always easy? No, it's not. Do we still struggle sometimes?

Absolutely. And yet it's easier than it was. I think you've got to make a game out of it; you've got to make it fun. You've got to set your goals high. **You've got to want something so bad that you're willing to go out there and pay the price to get it.** So many people say that they want to make millions of dollars, and yet they won't pay the price! That price, unfortunately, can be very steep, just like I told you with public speaking. It took years for me to get any good at it at all. And yes, it took years for me to learn how to write a sales letter. It took years to learn how to do *anything* that I do now. The same is true for all of the world's richest people. So, whatever it is that you want, you can have it. **If it's making millions of dollars in DRM, then that's exactly what we can do to help you.** *But you have to work hard at it.*

Recently Chris Lakey had a chance to speak at a political rally. There were maybe a couple hundred people in the room as he was getting ready to speak, and one of the other guys who was going to talk came over to Chris and said something like, "Don't be nervous." Chris just replied, "I'm not nervous at all. I'm excited. I'm looking forward to it." Chris didn't know if the guy was telling me him not to be nervous because he was nervous, or thought Chris looked nervous. But Chris has spoken to hundreds of people before, so it was no big deal for him. But had he been in that room with hundreds of people and had never been up in front of people before, he might have been scared to death to do that. **But as with everything else, it because much easier with repetition.**

Chapter Seven:

Magical Marketing Tricks

In this chapter, **I'm going to reveal some marketing tricks that pull in cash-paying customers like magic — faster and easier than you ever imagined possible.** The secrets I'll reveal here are may sound rather basic and simplistic, but I really do have to explain them... because although they seem like common sense, most people don't actually use them. As the saying goes, "One of the most uncommon things is common sense."

Give 'Em What They Want

The first magic marketing trick I'd like to discuss — and frankly, it may be the most magical marketing trick of all — **is speaking directly to the wants of your customer.** Now, you might say, "Okay, that sounds super-simplistic. But what does that actually mean, and how is it actually going to help me?"

Well, let me tell you, most people understand this concept — but they don't *do* it. And let's take realtors as an example. If I'm looking for a realtor to help me sell my home, I've got a specific want, right? I've got a problem, and the problem is that I have a house that I need help selling. So I'm going to go out try to find a realtor. Now, if you look at most realtors' advertising, does their headline say something like, "Are you desperately looking to sell your house in the next 30 days? If so, here's the solution..."

Absolutely not! A good 99.9% of realtors' ads don't do that; instead, most say something like "Mary Jones." "Todd Wilson." "Bob Franklin." These realtors put *their own names* as the headlines, and they slap their pictures up there. I can't tell you how many billboards I've driven by for realtors where you don't even know it's a realtor because, basically, it's a huge picture of somebody and their name and a slogan that says, "We're here for you." Well, okay, what are they "here for me" for? I may have a problem that you can solve. I may want to give you money. **But unless you're going to connect with me and let me know *how* you're going to help me, there's no way I'm going to be doing business with you.**

What I suggest is that you take yourself out of that equation. I realize that's going to be difficult for a lot of people, because whenever we do marketing we believe that we need to brand ourselves — that we need to put our face and our name out there. Well, let me turn that around. **If you're able to solve somebody's problem, they'll get to know you.** You'll be branded based on the result you're able to give them. Don't just throw your name and picture onto your marketing materials, hoping you'll gather a lot of business by building your brand. That's not how it works at all for small businesses. **Instead, connect with your customer, connect with your prospect, and determine what they really want.**

And let's go deeper than just that. What you want to do is to close your eyes and imagine that you *are* your prospect. **You want to imagine that you have the exact same experiences as a normal consumer of your products or services would have.** You want to imagine what their lives are like, the house that they live in, the income that they make, if they're married, if they're unmarried, what their daily life is like, what their schedule is like, what their other frustrations are like... **really put yourself in** *their* **shoes.** That's going to be very difficult for most marketers to do, because we're so used to saying, "Okay, we want to sell them something. We want to push something on them."

But that's a misconception. **What you *really* want to be in the business of is providing solutions; and the best way you can communicate with your prospects is by figuring out what their exact problem is and offering the ideal solution.** What perception do they have of that problem? If you can put yourself into their shoes and into their life and into their mindset, then you can speak exactly to that particular problem and offer a solution — and carry that a little bit further. You can also then determine where you need to be marketing.

So let's say, for example, that somebody has a particular problem and you've put yourself in their shoes. What that allows you to do is then project outwards and say, "Okay, I'm this person," and you may even give them a name so you can identify with the group as a whole. What you're going to do is say, "Okay, I'm Bob, the avatar of my target market. Here's my biggest problem. If I were suddenly motivated to take action to find a solution to my problem, what would I do? Where would I go? Would I call a friend? Would I go to the Yellow Pages? Would I go onto the Internet? If I went onto the Internet, where would I go? Would I go to Google? If I went to Google to do a search, what would the search terms be?"

Now, you have to realize that Bob's not looking for a particular product or provider; **he's looking for a solution to his problem, whatever form it might come in.** It might be different than an average marketer might think, so you've got to put yourself in the minds of prospects. Again, put yourself in their shoes at the exact time they have that problem, project yourself forward to see what actions they're taking, what they're looking for, **and then create a sales message that speaks directly to their wants.**

Let's go back to the realtor example. If they're looking to sell a house, what you want to say is, "Are you having a hard time finding a realtor you can trust to sell your house?" Or, "Would you like to sell your house in the next 30 days or less... guaranteed?" Or, "How would you like to start promoting your house today, within the next 30 minutes, and have it sold within the next 30 days... guaranteed... or I'll buy your house from you?" Something along those lines. If someone who was selling a home had those challenges and saw that headline above and beyond your name, they'd definitely be interested; **they'd be hooked because you're providing that precise solution. That can happen in any and every market, with any type of a prospect that has a problem.** Again, it sounds like a lot of common sense, but most people get away from that. We marketers like the excitement of product, and we like putting our names and our great sales messages out there. But the reality of the situation is that you can connect better with your prospects, make more sales, and create a better relationship by first putting yourself in the prospect's mind and then delivering exactly what they want in terms of the marketing message.

We have to pound this into our clients and potential joint venture partners over and over. Most people we work with come to us with specific products and services that they want to sell and that's all they want to talk about: "How can I get this product or service into the hands of the people that I want to sell it to?" And they have this crazy idea that everybody's going to just be as in love with what they're selling as much as they are. **That's hardly the case, so we tell people to start with the market first, not the product. That's the secret of our success.** If somebody said to me, "Hey, T.J., just give it to me on a 5 x 7 index card. What is it that really made you all of the millions of dollars?" **I would just tell them that it's all about empathy.**

You may already know my story, and it may be your story

too; in fact, most of the entrepreneurs in this field have a similar one. For years I sent away for every single get-rich-quick program I could find. I was on all of the mailing lists, and I got ripped off and lied to and cheated so many times. And then, when I finally did find a plan and a program that really truly worked and offered that to the millions of people in the opportunity market, **I knew their story and they knew ours. We were them and they were us. It's just that simple. You start with the market first.**

But it's hard to convince people of that. They feel it's only natural that it's all about the product first. But to succeed they have to get that out of their heads, because it's really about the product itself in a very small way. **The customer and their needs are first and foremost, followed by the benefits that they'll get from your product. To them, it's a solution, that's all.** It doesn't matter if it's a new system or a topical cream, as long as it works. Let me re-emphasize this: **You have to start with knowing what kinds of things your market is dealing with, not just in terms of their problems but in terms of what other people are selling to your target market.** What are they not providing that those people want? From that knowledge, you can create or find a product. There are all kinds of ways you can actually get a product into those people's hands, but you always have to start with the group of people that you want to sell to, and then determine what their challenges are and what kinds of products they really want the most. Look for people with a huge problem that they need solved, a huge challenge that they can't face alone. If there's tons of pressure in the marketplace, that means there's a huge opportunity for you to fill that need, meet that demand, and make a lot of money in the process. **It all starts not with the product, but with the prospect.**

Now, someone with a business degree would probably say, at this point, "Hey, that's way too simple, guy." Well, you know

what? **The simplest things are usually the most effective.**
Most of us try to make marketing and business a lot more
complicated than it has to be. It's all about all complex theories,
concepts, constructs, and elaborate accounting and analysis,
right? Well, no. **Ultimately, business is about delivering
solutions to people who have problems. Period.** Really
knowing that in your heart of hearts is a powerful thing, because
if you can provide a group of people with a workable solution to
one of their problems, it's going to make a real connection —
and you're going to make so much money by offering them that
solution that you'll be blown away.

Let's take a look at a large, ravenous market: the weight
loss market (no pun intended). By and large, these people don't
care about the name of your product, who you are, or how long
you've been in business. *They care about results.* They want to
lose weight, as fast and as easily as possible. So if you have a
product that delivers that solution, you're going to make a good
connection with that market, because they *want* the solution.
Again, it all boils down to the need to start with the prospect, not
the product. **You can develop a product once you know what
people want.** For heaven's sake, don't be like those people who
spend weeks or months or, heaven forbid, *years* creating a
product, then they take it to the market they think is going to buy
it and, BOOM! Nobody does, and they're left broke and
scratching their heads, wondering, "Okay, why didn't this
work?" It's simply because they never realized they were going
about it all wrong.

It makes more sense to find what the market wants, and
then give it to them. To some people it seems exploitative; that
may be why some people aren't doing it. **But you're in
business to give people exactly what they want, not what you
want or think they should need.** No matter how good it is for
them, you can't force people to buy and use your product.

Now, entrepreneurs tend to be very smart people, even though they sometimes do stupid things and tend to complicate everything. **So keep it simple: boil it down until you can see the biggest frustrations in the marketplace, and how can you solve them instantly.** At M.O.R.E., Inc., we're developing products and services that are designed for business owners. We know what services we want to sell to them, yet it's not about what *we* want to sell to *them*. It's about what they're looking for, and it's about understanding their biggest problems. You should try to match the two as closely as you can.

What people really want, in a very general sort of way, is relief from some form of pain they're in. Let's go back to the weight-loss industry. People who want to lose weight are in great emotional trauma; it's all they think about. Similarly, the people who really want to make a lot of money think about little else. They're frustrated, and there's a certain amount of tension here. **The market that we're trying to reach with our business products represents anywhere from 12-30 million people who own small- to mid-size business.** They have all kinds of problems and frustrations and pressures — things that keep them awake at night, that get them out of bed in the morning, that just drive them crazy. So what we have to do is develop products and services that are centered around their biggest problems, and our degree of being able to do that determines how much money we're going to get from them. Simple as that. And it does sound simple; **but I don't want you to think that this is easy.** There's nothing easy about it; it requires lots of hard work.

And yet, once you know how simple it is, that helps keep you focused. That's really the key. You start with this simple concept and realize, "Okay, I've got to dig down and figure out what my market wants." Now, saying that is very simplistic, but actually doing it is a whole another deal. You're talking about interviewing or surveying people to understand what they want. One of the things I've gotten away from that I'm starting to do more of again is really talking to my market, and I hear this from many of my colleagues as well. Whenever you grow in any particular business, the level between you and your customers and prospects grows. You may think you've still got an idea of what your market wants, when, in reality, you might have no clue. Let's be honest — if it's 5, 10 or 20 years since you've been in their shoes, some of that intensity has died down.

So what my colleagues and I do nowadays is speak directly to our own customers and clients at seminars. One of my colleagues, Jeff Gardner, makes it a habit to go to seminars similar to his own that are being sold to other people in his market, and just talk to the people there. He's also been doing surveys to people on his mailing list where he asks directly, "What are you interested in? What's your biggest challenge? What's your biggest problem?" He even tells them, "Look, I'm looking for a problem outside of what my market or what my company can offer you." **Now, my company and his both develop products and opportunities that help people quit their jobs and work for themselves.** So Jeff will ask people, "Okay, I want you to tell me all your problems. If it's back pain, it's relationship issues or whatever, tell me, because I want to have such a great understanding of where you're at that I'm able to develop solutions to those problems." As a result, he's getting a lot of information that's deeper than he expected. It's helping him develop products, services, and opportunities that really match with the market. **That's the value of doing some legwork to actually connect with the market.** So, again, a simple concept; but believe me, it'll pay off over time.

Crushing the Competition

Once you're in the market, helping people solve their

problems, **you've got to do something about all those other pesky people trying to do the same thing, so you can make as much money as you can.** Well, that's easier than you might think: I know of one method, courtesy of the aforementioned Jeff Gardner, that can quadruple your profits at the expense of your competitors. **All you have to do is give away one free item.** This item is so powerful that you have the opportunity to literally blow your competition out of the water and dominate your market. By now, you're probably wondering, "Okay, so what *is* this one free thing? Is it a CD? Is it a report? What is it?"

What is it? **It's education. It's information.**

Again, it's a simple concept, but let me explain exactly how powerful, how absurdly magical, this concept can be. A lot of marketers are guilty of giving you all the sizzle and none of the steak. We get you hyped up. We tell you how great a product is, offering all the bullet points and a great headline. We tease until you're drooling, you want the product so bad. Then we let you buy the product and you rush to get it.

That's how a lot of marketers work. But the truth is, you can crush your competition and make much, much more money if you'll also deliver part of the steak during your spiel — not just the sizzle. **If, for example, you're willing to give up some of your best information to your prospects before they pay you any money, you have the ability to create a strong bond with the market, because no one else is giving them any meat-and-potatoes information.** But let's say you're willing to give them an actual trick, a technique, something that will work for them before they buy from you. What will that do to the prospect? **That gets them to want to buy the product from you.** Why? Well, when somebody sees a sales letter, whether it's online, through direct-mail, or even as a full-page ad in a magazine, all they know is what you're saying about the product; they don't have the ability to sample it. They don't have the ability to match the quality of what you say you're going to deliver with your marketing message. So in their own head they've got to make that decision: "Okay, is this person hyping it up too much? Are they really going to deliver?" In some cases they're sitting on the fence wondering, "Should I or shouldn't I?" **If you're willing to give up some of that valuable information, you're going to make the buying process a lot easier.** They'll be able to gauge the quality of the information you have to give to them; and if you've got great information, they're likely to go ahead and purchase.

Now, a lot of marketers understand this concept of giving a little information, hoping to hook you and pull you in, **but they don't want to give you the best stuff.** They want to save the best stuff for the big product, for the big seminar, for the big home study course. **But I think that's counterproductive.** What I would recommend is that you give away the *best* stuff free. **Take that one technique that really works, and give it to the prospect before they actually buy.** You may think that that sounds insane, but consider the psychology of the prospect. They believe that if you're giving away this solid gold information for free, then the information they have to pay for will be worth even more. That's likely to push the sale ahead.

This isn't about keeping stuff back. A lot of marketers will hold everything back and say, "No, no, no. Before you can get any of my stuff, you've got to hand over some money." So what I'm saying to do is counter-intuitive. **Now, don't give them *all* your best info, but do give them a big bite of it.** Share that with them. Show them you trust them, and that will prove to them that everything else you've got is high-quality information. It's a great concept that gives you the ability to create a bond with your prospect that I would say 98% of other marketers simply aren't willing to try. **It gives you the ability to crush your competition and more than quadruple your sales**

because you're standing above everybody else in your market. You're doing something that nobody else is doing. So what your prospect is saying is, "Okay, this person is willing to give me the best of the best information. Obviously, all their other information is great, so I'm going to spend my money with them instead of all these other people that refuse to give me any information." It's a very simple method, but it has the ability to really increase your sales and thereby crush your competition.

Our Automatic Recruiting System is a DRM system we've developed that gives away a $495 program called "20/20 Wealth Vision." **And yet we're giving it away absolutely free, with no strings, no gimmicks, no tricks, no fine print, no cost... no nothing!** It's available on the website for free, and then if people want to pay a $5 fee to help cover some of our costs, they can get the MP-3 version. If they want to spend a bit more money and get all nine audio CDs, it's pretty much at our cost. We don't make any profit on that. **We're just trying to blow people away!** Similarly, another of our programs offers the "Part-Time Riches" program — $4,529 worth of products condensed to MP-3 format. There are no catches, though there's a condition attached to the offer; the programs are worth $4,529 and are free as a bonus with a specific sale that our distributors are making. **We even let people keep the free programs if they return the product that's part of the offer.** In this way, we differentiate ourselves from the competition. Most people will never figure this out, and the ones who do are usually too afraid to do it. They just can't get their minds wrapped around the concept that people would want to buy if what they got from you for free was of the highest quality. And incidentally, on the flipside, people will be inclined to choose not to do business with you if what they get free from you is garbage.

Now, I can see where they're coming from, because think of it this way: You don't go into many restaurants and find that the cheeseburger costs $29.50, while the filet mignon is only $1.95. That doesn't happen; the highest-priced stuff is the best stuff. **So you've got to make that mental shift to use this great strategy.** It's something that Hollywood figured out long ago. If you see a movie trailer on TV and then go see the movie, a lot of times you're like, "Okay, I feel like I already saw everything, because all the best parts were in the trailer." In other words, they give away all the best parts, and that gets you to go see the movie. If that two-minute trailer was of the boring scenes from the middle of the movie, where it was dragging a little, you might be thinking, "Boy, I've got other things I could be doing instead of sitting here watching this horrible scene." No, they give away the best part, the high-action scenes, the things that make you sit on the edge of your seat. That's what gets you to go to the movie.

When you're selling your product, you can do the same thing. **Give them the best stuff free, and that will make them salivate for the rest of what you have.** That's not to say that the rest of what you have is trash; I'm just saying to pick out the best of the best stuff. Pick the things that are going to make your customer salivate the most. Deliver on that information free, and that will get them to come running to you with their wallets open, ready to give you whatever you ask to get the rest of the benefits you're guaranteeing through your offer.

Here are two strategies you can use to put this concept into action. Let's say you've got a print product, an eBook, or something similar that you're selling. **One of the most powerful things you can do is give prospects a free chapter or a free excerpt from that product.** Recently, Jeff Gardner had a book that was selling very successfully online. It wasn't written by him, but by a marketing expert by the name of Vincent James. The book is called *The 12 Month Millionaire*. Well, on Jeff's website, he gave away the first chapter absolutely free. Now, one of the things he requested was that the prospects gave him their names and email addresses; and then he emailed them the first chapter, word for word. Now why would Jeff do that? Because he knew that after they finished reading that very first chapter, which offered a lot of information, they were going to want to read the second, the third, the fourth, and on and on — every chapter of that book. So he wasn't afraid to give away one chapter, because Jeff knew that by giving them that valuable information, an actual part of that product, would make them want to purchase the rest.

A second strategy pertains specifically to email. A lot of people are overwhelmed with spam emails. They've got so many coming in that they often go straight into the trash. Well, here's a secret that can get your email not only opened up, but have people looking forward to it: **Hand out valuable information in every email.** For example, give them a strategy, a technique, a trick, something that will actually benefit them. This will make them open all your emails, and will actively encourage them to go to your website or call you in order to get the other valuable info you offer. **You basically train your list so that when you send them something, they open it up right away.**

Again, **it's all about separating yourself from the competition.** One of my mentors, Russ von Hoelscher, tells a great story about a sandwich shop that consulted with him years ago. They said, "Russ, our business is just going down the drain. Although we make the best sandwiches in San Diego, the neighborhood our little store is in has sort of... well, let's just say it's turned seedy." All of a sudden the prostitutes had started hanging out in that neighborhood, and it was full of "massage parlors" and those movie theaters that don't show family films. The whole neighborhood had gone to hell. And yet, this guy either owned his real estate or was locked into a long-term lease, and couldn't get out of it. However, within a couple of blocks of his sandwich shop were all these high-rise office buildings.

So after Russ sampled his sandwiches, he told this guy, "Here's what you have to do…" It was a simple idea, based on exactly what I'm talking about, and it completely turned that business around. All he did was hire these attractive, well-dressed young women, and they delivered samples every day, right before noon, to those office buildings. They were very clean, neat, and professional, and they would give out samples of the sandwiches along with a little menu card, and answer any questions. **They gave away hundreds of dollars worth of free food every single week — and yet they got back thousands of dollars worth of repeat business from people who sampled the product,** loved the sandwiches, and were willing to go through neighborhoods that they wouldn't necessarily want to go through if there wasn't something at the other end waiting for them that was really delicious. Eventually, the shop developed a delivery system where it brought the sandwiches right to the offices. I always thought that was one of the greatest success stories I've ever heard.

Now, a lot of people just don't get the point of that story because they think, "Well, I don't run a sandwich shop. I can't pass out sandwiches." But that's the great thing about the information business: **We have the ability to get information to people very inexpensively.** It's true for just about any business you're in. If I were a realtor, I could offer a report on the ten things to definitely not do when selling your home, or ten things to understand before you buy a new home. It's the same with carpet cleaners, plumbers, or any business you're in: **You can give away some information or education to your prospects before they actually purchase from you.** By doing that, you're able to make that connection, set yourself apart, and pull prospects in better than everybody who's just showing them the marketing and the advertising.

Earlier, I mentioned that a lot of realtors use ads that basically tell you their name, and that's it. Their name doesn't offer a big benefit, does it? Obviously, there's some benefit to having name recognition, and you want to be known in your industry. But people just scanning, looking for a realtor, want a benefit — and the advertisers don't give you one. I think a lot of markets are like that. A lot of the folks running ads in the Yellow Pages could do themselves a *huge* service just by having someone who knows marketing rewrite their ad and **focus on a benefit: offering some giveaway that could draw attention to their ad** and make it look different than all the others are running next to it.

But people don't even think that way. Unfortunately, they get bound into their particular market. **They forget that they have all of these competitors, and forget that they have to do something strong to differentiate themselves.** They're running with the herd and wondering why they're not getting good results. Well, sometimes you have to do the thing that's counter-intuitive, something different than everybody else, so you can really stand out above your competition.

Competing on Price

Most business owners seem to think that competing on price is a great way to make money. But you know what? **Competing on price can absolutely kill your business.** It makes no sense, because there's usually somebody in any market who's either crazy or doesn't understand business, so they're happy to keep lowering their prices until they even drive themselves out of business.

So what you want to compete on is everything else: service, quality, speed, ease of purchase and use, customer experience, etc. Create a brainstorming sheet for every aspect of your business, and find ways you can deliver a 'wow' experience to the people in your market. **Determine how you can go above and beyond in everything you do,** in terms of delivering whatever you're offering, so that that person says, "Wow! This company is phenomenal. I'm glad I'm doing business with them!"

In any market, you're going to have price shoppers. There's no way around that. But at the same time, you also have people who buy on experience, quality, and speed. What I would recommend is this: **Don't try to sell to your entire market.** Put aside the people who buy based on price and say to yourself, "Okay, I'm going to give up all these people to the competitors who are happy to compete on price, and let them drive each other out of business. From today forward, **I'm not competing on price.** That part of the market is invisible to me. From this day forward, I'm competing on everything else I can deliver to my customers and prospects: that 'wow' experience."

The reason you want to do that is because **you're going to build up a clientele that's more loyal than if you were competing on price.** Those people aren't loyal; the *only* thing they're interested in is price, so they're going to jump around from company to company looking for the best price. If you get away from them and deliver the best service, in the best time, with the best quality, you can build up a bond where those people will come back and do business with you repeatedly, for years to come. But above and beyond that, if you give somebody a 'wow' experience, do they want to keep it to themselves? No! **They want to tell other people.** They *love* to tell other, "Hey, guess what? I just had this crazy experience with this company. I bought this product and they hand-delivered it on a silver platter." Or, "They sent it overnight, wrapped up in a red bow." Or, "They sent along a box of chocolates with it," or whatever that 'wow' experience is for your particular market. People are going to share that, and you're going to generate more business, free of charge.

Of course, a lot of people in any business think, "Okay, we want our customers to go out and get us more customers." Well, if you're just doing an okay job and people are kind of satisfied, they're not going to go out talk about your company. **But when there's a 'wow' experience, they're much more willing to share that with a friend.** It doesn't matter what business you're in; whether you're selling information products, cleaning carpets, or showing real estate, you need to brainstorm some 'wow' experiences. How can you really impress people? And let me tell you, it can be with things that are very, very simple.

Let me share an example from Jeff Gardner, who lives in Dallas. A few years back, he hired a plumber to come to his home and fix a clogged sink. This was a new plumber, because he'd been through four or five — and these people would come in, be shoddily dressed, and make a mess. Jeff was never really happy with that, so he'd always move on the next company, and the next. Well, this new fellow came into Jeff's house pristinely dressed, and he was thoughtful enough to put on little booties so he didn't track dirt into Jeff's house. Now, that stuck in Jeff's mind forever! Everyone else had always tracked in dirt and leaves and twigs and soiled the carpet, and they never gave a damn. Well, Jeff got a great vibe off this gentleman right off the bat. He came in, did exactly what he said he was going to do at a great price, and gave Jeff a business card and a refrigerator magnet before he left. **Jeff had just had a phenomenal experience!** So guess who he called the next time he had plumbing problems? A different company? No, he called that company again — and then he called them again and again, just because of a few simple things that company does better than every other plumbing company in the area. **He's recommended them to other people since.**

So just think of ways that you can give people a 'wow' experience. **All you have to do to profit, in many cases, is to leave your customers with a better impression.** It doesn't have to cost you a lot; you just have to do the small things right, and you'll be rewarded with their repeat business. At the same time, keep away from competing on price — because it can destroy your business. **Remember, people who look just for the lowest price aren't long-term, loyal customers.** Price is something that annoys me when people talk about it, because usually if you compete on price, it means you're cutting costs somewhere. Obviously, every business exists to make a profit; but if you're making a small enough profit that you're competing on price, you're going to have competitors that will drive you into the ground. Eventually you'll get to where there's no profit left.

No Work, No Hassle, Baby!

Here's one of my favorite magical marketing methods: **We call it the "no work, no hassle way to making extra profits instantly."** I know that sounds like a lot of hype, but here's the way to do it: **Simply include an upsell whenever you're doing any type of marketing.** An upsell is something extra you offer to someone who's already committed to the buying process. This is how the people on those infomercials work. Let's say you call up to buy that cool rotisserie or the pasta maker or Ginsu knives or whatever it is. While they've got you on the line taking all your information, before you hang up they try to add something else on. "Well here's our Discount Buyers Club," or "Here's extra-fast shipping," or "Here's a monthly membership to a magazine or membership site," or any number of things. **The reason I call this a "no work, no hassle" way to make extra profits instantly is because they've already committed to buying something from you, so all you're doing is adding one extra step.** It doesn't cost you any extra work or money, assuming you already have the product available.

When you make that offer, you're going to have a certain percentage of people who will happily add on that extra item to their order. **That automatically gives you additional money with no additional marketing costs.** Think about it: the marketing costs were already there. You've already paid to get that prospect to a website, or to send them your direct-mail letter, or have them come to your Yellow Pages ad. They've already decided to buy — so when you offer them something else, there's no additional cost. On the Internet, one of the ways that we use this method is that after they click the "Buy" button, we take them to an upsell page where they can take the basic or deluxe package. Offline you can do that on an order form. "Oh, by the way, we've also got this brand new audio CD," or "We've got this brand new DVD set. How would you like to add that to your order?" It's all about finding that thing that goes with whatever you're selling, and it's such a quick, easy technique.

As I mentioned earlier, we recently developed some products that go out to business owners, and the product we want to sell the most of costs about $5,000. Well, a lot of people who are brand new to us don't trust us enough yet to give us $5,000, and we know that. **We know that trust has to be earned, so we use a kind of stair-step method where we first try to sell them more inexpensive products.** However, there are some people within those groups of prospects who are like me — I'm the person who'll just spend five grand and take a risk. **So we put that $5,000 offer right there on every order form,** telling them to call a special number, because we know that a certain percentage of people will. **That's instant cash in our pocket when they do.**

If you've got an expensive upsell, you might want to take them to a dead-end voice mailbox where you can give them a five-minute phone message where you explain it a little more. But it's been proven time and time again that you don't even need to explain it much if it's self-explanatory. Maybe you've got an upsell that's a couple hundred bucks, even, that just says, "Hey, we've got this package. Here's what it is..." You give them a paragraph about it on the order form and give them the title of the product or service, and tell them what the regular price is. But if they check this box on the form, you'll add it to their order for only *this* much. **An upsell like that can put you in the profits much faster.**

CHAPTER EIGHT:

It's All About the Systems

The theme for this chapter is how to systemize your business. Systems may seem kind of boring, but the fact is that you need to be organized, and you need to have processes in place to help you bring in the money as smoothly and as speedily as possible. In this lesson, we'll look at **three ways to get those systems up and running.** I'm also going to talk about the leverage blueprint; that is, **how you can harness the efforts of others to unlock your dreams.** Finally, I'm going to wrap it up with the **little-known secrets to setting the stage for huge paydays** — why some get a lot, while others get just a little.

Systemize from Day One

First of all, **you need to find something great that you're going to use as your lure.** After all, you can't market something if you don't have something to market! **So again, scrutinize the marketplace carefully, and determine what your market wants.** If you don't want to create your own product, find an existing product that offers something that's very much in demand. For example: if you're with the Direct-Response Network, you know we've got a great product there. Next, look at the timing of the marketplace, and make sure that your product lines up with what's happening there. **You can make some serious money with timing.**

Make sure that your products are supported well, too. I always say, "Look to the field." If you're involved in something or you're thinking about getting involved in something, a good way to determine whether or not that's the right direction is to **look out in the field and see if other people are already making money with it.** If you can find a handful of people who are making $100,000 a month in the program, then it's a workable program and you can make some money. As my colleague Eric Bechtold always says, **"Success leaves clues."** Looking for those clues is a good, cheap way to test whether or not you've got the right product.

Once you've identified your product, **the second step is to generate your message.** How are you going to take that product to market? How are you going to communicate it? Eric uses something he calls the **"Seven Steps to Magnetic Communication,"** and I'd like to share them with you. These are the things you have to do in order to really communicate with people effectively and get them excited. **NUMBER ONE is to look at your product and identify your big promise.** A good way to closely examine your product is to take out a package of note cards, and list, one by one, your product's benefits — that is, everything it has to offer. Don't look at it from a standpoint of physical attributes; write only the benefits on your cards. When you're finished doing that, thumb through those cards, **pick your number one idea,** and move that to the top. **That's what you're going to build your strategy around.** If you're having a hard time figuring out what your big promise is, then you've got the wrong product. **That product *must* have something that makes it stand out.** If it's hard for you to determine what it is, it's going to be hard for those you're trying to sell it to to figure out why they need to be paying attention to it.

NUMBER TWO, once you've identified your big promise, start painting the picture. This is where you **take all**

those other cards you set aside and use them as an outline
for your sales material. One benefit may serve as a headline in
your copy, or as supporting copy that fleshes out those ideas so
people understand why they're important.

NUMBER THREE, give them proof. A good way to do
this is through social validation: success stories, case studies, or
testimonials. In any case, you want to figure out some way of
proving you've got the right product that can offer the solutions
everybody's looking for. You want to give them proof to make
it real. If there's no proof, they're not going to buy it.

NUMBER FOUR, you want to build exclusivity. Why is
your product unique? Why do they need to buy this from you?
Why can't they just go out and find this from somebody else?
Make them feel like this is something that they can't get
anywhere else, so they want to buy it from you. People buy
what feels exclusive, what feels exciting and important... so you
want to build that into your offer.

NUMBER FIVE, you want to build urgency, so that
people act now. Give them special bonuses. Create limited
group sizes. There are a lot of different tricks and strategies in
direct-response for building urgency; but here's the reality.
You're using the big promise to get people excited, to get them
to focus on it. You're using all this other stuff I've just talked
about to give them the story and to paint the picture. And then,
you're using this sense of urgency to close them on the spot,
because if you can't get them to take quick action, there's a
good chance they're not going to take action at all.

NUMBER SIX, you're going to re-state that big promise
and really drive it home. And then, NUMBER SEVEN,
you're going to build in risk reversal. Risk reversal is very,
very important, and you've seen this all over the place. There's
one word that will make this all gel for you, and that's

"guarantee." Your goal here is get them to focus on the offer while taking away all the negative aspects they may consider, like "Oh no, I've got to spend $400 to get this product." You've got to reverse that risk and make them understand that, "Hey, if I try this for 30 days and I'm not happy, I can get my money back!" or whatever the guarantee may be. That will help you in the end.

Before we move on to the next subject for this chapter, leverage, let's review a bit. **First, you've got to identify that product and then generate your message, using the seven points I've just outlined.** That, I think, is the real the starting point of your entire business. If you've got a product and can't think of a big promise, you're probably barking up the wrong tree altogether. Risk reversal is also a big thing: you've got to make people understand that there's no risk in taking on your product. Now, some companies don't have guarantees at all; they're afraid that by having a guarantee, people will take advantage of them. But we like to say that you can never have too outrageous a guarantee. **The more outrageous the guarantee, the more it stacks the situation in your prospect's favor.** The more you can make it appear that all the risk is on you and none of it's on them, the more likely it is that someone is going to go ahead and place their order.

We've had guarantees that, under certain restrictions, gave our customers double the money back that they spent with us, and that was on a rather expensive offer. We put it on the line, and while we had several stipulations they had to agree to before that happened, it made the offer all the more attractive to them. **And by the way, it's better, in most cases, if you make it as easy as possible for your clients to get their money back if they're not happy.** A standard 30-day guarantee is good, but having a guarantee where you tell them, "Hey, under any circumstances, you can get a full 100% refund, no questions asked," makes people feel more comfortable. **It makes them feel like there's very little chance that they're risking anything at all.**

And again, **the product you're promoting has to be hot.** I've mentioned that in the first four years after we started our company, we brought in more than ten million dollars. And everyone wants to know, what was the secret? In truth, there was no single secret; it was a combination of many different factors, including the fact that we'd struggled for so many years and refused to quit. **Every time we thought we were failing, we were actually learning something.** So by the time we'd failed 50 times, even though we had never made any serious money, we had learned a lot about what *didn't* work. But if there was one thing besides all the experience that made all the difference in the world, **it was the fact that finally we hit on the right idea at the right time. That's so important.**

I see entrepreneurs out there trying to sell what *they* love, not necessarily what the market loves. We've got some good friends who are wasting their time and money selling things that nobody finds exciting but them. There's no market for that; so one of the best things you can do is either partner with someone who already has a hot product or service, or copy something that works for someone else. That may seem a little ruthless, but I'm not telling you to copy it exactly; no, put your own spin on it and make it *better*. **That's basically how we got started.** We took two programs that were already working for others and combined them to create our own very profitable program.

In order to succeed, you've got to get on the other side of the cash register. Stop thinking like a consumer; start thinking like a marketer. All those steps are things that *all* successful marketers are using to various degrees. Some are doing a better job than others, **but you'll never recognize that until and unless you start studying their sales material.** First of all, don't throw it away, and stop calling it junk mail. Get on the right mailing lists, and look at it from a marketer's point of view rather than a consumer's point of view — and you'll start seeing these things used. The untrained eye will never see these things; but if you're aware of them, you can start using them yourself.

The Leverage Blueprint

My second secret for this chapter involves **harnessing the efforts of others to unlock your dreams.** The key here is that you don't get rich by yourself. If you try, you're limited to the money that's in your wallet for marketing, you're limited to your knowledge on how to promote things, and you're limited to how much time you can work every day. Most people who try to get rich on their own fail miserably, and the reason is that they're not leveraging the efforts of others. They're only using their own limited resources. **Finding the right position of leverage is the ultimate solution to the marketing equation.**

Now, how have we used this concept with the previous secret? I just told you how to find an offer and how to develop a good message, because **that lure is how you catch your fish — that is, how you generate your customer base.** Once you get one thing working well and you've got a bunch of people coming in, you're going to start putting all those people in a database, such as an Excel spreadsheet. You're keeping the names of all those people organized, in such a way that you can sort them by various characteristics.

And then here's what you do: Instead of just putting all your people in a program and saying, "Now go out and figure out how to do it for yourself," you tell them, "Hey, I've got it all figured out. I'm going to give you access to the same things I'm doing, and you can do them yourself." **That creates a snowball effect** in your business, because you went through the effort of finding the good lure that brought in those people, and then you're giving them access to your methods and secrets. You're the gatekeeper here. You're not worried about them jeopardizing your copyrights; in fact, you're not worried about your intellectual property at all. Why is that? Because every time they use them, you're leveraging their efforts. They're putting their money into a mailing, or putting up their own websites, or whatever you're giving them. The easier you can make it for somebody to make you money, the better off you're going to be. So if you get as many people as you can and make it as easy as possible for others to make you money while they make themselves money, guess what? Your profits will explode!

The easiest way to rise to the top is on the shoulders of a bunch of other people who are putting their effort into building their own businesses. We tell people this all the time in network marketing. The only advantage of network marketing is leverage, the fact they've built a leverage model for you. If you're not a big fan of network marketing, then go to a Master Distributorship, where you have the rights to sell other people the rights to sell a product. There are many different ways to build leverage; lots of different ways to put more money in your pocket without having to invest more of your time and money to make it happen. The biggest money earners in the world, the Bill Gateses and the Donald Trumps, are leveraging the efforts of other people every single day. Think about the way these guys are making money. Donald Trump isn't building skyscrapers by himself, right? He's got everybody else doing it. He's figured out a way to sit at the top of that big tower and make money by leveraging the efforts of all these other people. If you want to follow in the footsteps of the most successful people, you'll take this leverage blueprint and put it to work for yourself.

That's one of the secrets to our success. If somebody were

to put a gun to my head and demand, "Give me your whole secret in less than five minutes!" this is what I'd tell him. It would be that simple. Look, in the opportunity market there are literally millions of people looking for a way to make money. All they really need are three things, and we've made millions of dollars over the years by providing them with a wide variety of different programs and opportunities containing these three basic ingredients, some of which I've already talked about. **Number One, they need some type of product to sell. Number Two, they need some type of sales material to sell that product with, whether that's postcards or direct-mail packages or websites. And Number Three, they need a cohesive marketing system that ties everything all together.** In less than five minutes, that's how our company has generated more than $110,000,000 in direct-marketing revenue over the years. Our goal is to do everything possible to help them make the largest amount of money possible, and that's how we make our money. **So we're helping them, but we're helping ourselves at the same time.** It really doesn't get any more complicated than that. We've been doing that since 1988 in various ways. Everything we do is wrapped up in providing those three things in some form.

When you've built an organized collection of all your prospects, which basically takes the form of a mailing list, you've got the ultimate marketing control. Otherwise, you've got to find a group of people to mail to or to send your offer to. You've got to have a group of leads somehow, so **you've got to do lead generation; you've got to do something to get those leads.** Sometimes that means you can joint-venture with other people if you've got a product. You can leverage your product and find other people with a list to sell to. **But once you've got a list, you will have a never-ending revenue stream;** because if you've got a list of responsive buyers, then all of a sudden you've got tremendous leverage. People will come to you saying, "I've got a hot product, and your list would be perfect for it," and all you have to do is take their materials, mail them to your list and you've got orders coming in.

If you've got a mailing list of people that have bought from you, and you've built a relationship with them, **there's almost no question about whether you'll make money every time you mail to that list, because those people know you, like you, and trust you.** That can provide you with a never-ending revenue stream. And it doesn't take a big list, either. Some people we know have made millions of dollars with lists of fewer than 1,000 people. I have friends who've made fortunes with lists of fewer than 300 people. Focusing on building a list is probably one of the most important things you can do.

The Third Secret

There are a lot of people pretending to be marketers who don't really understand how to make a lot of money quickly. And the secret is, **you don't do it overnight.** You don't just come up with an idea, and BOOM, $100,000 comes falling out of the sky (if only!). Nope, it doesn't work like that. **Making money effectively requires systems.** This includes building a list of people to make offers to, as I've discussed previously. Once you reach this point, you're at a stage where your list is basically "stored energy" for you. Your customers are sitting there, and you have to start building rapport with them. A good way to do this to offer newsletters; this lets you communicate with people frequently. You get them on conference calls, too. And again, one of the things that's most important to understand here is that you don't take advantage of your database. **Everything you do has to be sincere, and you have to show them that you have an honest desire and are you're passionate about helping them.** They've got to feel that, because one of the things that will keep the people on your list from buying is if they feel you're not sincere, or not putting your best foot forward.

What you need to understand is that **customers in all markets want somebody to do everything for them.** They're always looking for guidance and direction, and they're always looking for that magic bullet, something or someone that's going to provide them with a neat solution to their problems. The neat thing about having a database is, now you're in a situation where you can communicate with people who are looking to be communicated with, looking for solutions, looking for a leader they can follow to achieve their desires, dreams, and goals. **You've got a leg up because you used that lure, you made that initial sale, and you generated this list.** You need to continue to use that lure until it stops working, and then you find another lure.

The whole goal here is to continue to pile people in. Now, again, I've told you that some marketers don't understand this; they just go out with a sales letter to the unwashed masses and expect to make a bunch of money. But, really, you don't make your money like that. **You make your money on what we call the "back-end."** That is, you take a list of people you've communicated with, that you've established a rapport with, and then come back with other offers that meet their needs. In order to help you determine that, you need to analyze your list based on what people have purchased. What lures have you used? What was the big promise in each case? What are the attributes that sold them in the first place? That's what you're going to use as a determiner when looking for other opportunities, products, or services to plug into. **The more complementary those offers are to their original purchase, the more money you're going to make.**

In a perfect environment, you're going to start with very little, and generate this list by finding a lure to which people are attracted. **You start piling people into your database.** Then you're going to go ahead and start communicating to them with a paper newsletter, an email newsletter, periodic telephone events, or a mix of these and other things. **You're going to just stay in contact, keeping your name in their minds.** As the list gets bigger and bigger, eventually you'll get to critical mass where you've got such a large group of people that you're in the position for big paydays.

Some people brag about things like, "Oh, I was able to do a $100,000 in one sales letter." "I did a million dollars with one big push." Well, that was all stored energy that they tapped into. They "unleashed" all of that. Think about the Hoover Dam; think about all that concrete cracking open and the water rushing out in a huge tidal wave. In a way, that's what they're doing. All that stored energy is being released on that offer, and money comes piling in as a result. **Now, think about the power of being in that situation — continuously having the lure, continuously developing a list, continuously staying in touch with that list.** And then you get into a position where all you're doing is looking out in the marketplace, finding great ideas and opportunities, plugging them in, and those big paydays come on a frequent basis. **Pretty soon you can do one a month or so, and you've got all the money that you've ever wanted.**

Again, it all stems from the system I just told you about. That's pretty much the cycle that you go through, and the power, the *gold*, really is in that list. So start taking those steps I've outlined in this chapter. And no, it won't be perfect the first time out; but as a friend of ours, well-known marketer Dan Kennedy, likes to say: **"It doesn't have to be good, just good enough."** This is especially true when you're tying your first lure on the line and getting ready to throw it out there, trying to attract your first customers. Don't worry about polishing it up until it's the best thing since sliced bread; you're going to fall forward, if you will. You're going to try a few things that are going to work a little... and they may not work to the best of your ability. **But you're going to hone your skills as you move forward, so you'll keep moving down to road. Forward, not backward.**

And here's something I'd like to point out: **Once you have a large, stable group of customers who like you, respect you, and trust you, it's going to be hard to fail.** I think that most marketers don't realize just how insatiable their customers really are. I think a lot of people are afraid to push too hard. When I was younger, I would worry that I was trying to sell too much stuff to my customers. My biggest fear was that they were going to feel I was trying to push too many products and services at them, and they were going to get turned off and not want to do business with me anymore. Now, quite frankly, the only thing I concern myself with is that we're not offering *enough* stuff to them. Because the fact is, if they're not buying from us, they're going to buy from somebody else. **People who are serious about making money are particularly insatiable, and they like looking at new opportunities constantly.** That's one of the reasons we continue to come up with all kinds of new opportunities for them, because that's what they like.

Too many people are afraid of making additional sales to their clients, and I think that's why they focus too much on selling to a customer the first time, and too little on re-selling to them. **Dear Reader, *do not* worry about the possibility of offending your clients. The reality is, you can't mail to them too much.** There's an enormous amount of discretionary money being spent in this country every year, on all kinds of products and services. Even though the economy is tight, and people say they're broke all the time, **they *will* spend money on things they really want.** It doesn't matter whether we're in a good economy or a bad economy. People are continuing to spend money like they have a never-ending supply, **and if you don't**

get your share, somebody else will — count on it.

And when you're talking about discretionary income, remember, you're competing with all kinds of entertainment choices: the latest book or movie, dinner at a restaurant, or the purchase of a $30,000 car versus a $15,000 car. In order to get the biggest possible share of that discretionary money, **you need to constantly remind your clients that they should be doing business with you.** And again, it all goes back to the list.

One of the first points I talked about in this chapter was identifying what the big benefit is — that big thing that your prospects are looking for. You've already filled it once by giving them the initial sale; **so now it's just a matter of continuing to find other products and services,** either by developing them yourself, licensing products, or engaging in Joint Venturing with other people. **Then you go back to your list and let them know about new opportunities, products, and services that you have available to them.** If you've done a good job of building your list, then every time you offer something, a portion of that list will decide that they want to spend money on you.

And by the way, **a list has a shelf life.** If you're a timid marketer, if you're afraid of mailing offers, if you're fearful you're going to make your clients upset if you send them another offer... then that list *will* go bad. **If that list isn't cultivated and maintained, if you don't continue with the relationship, the relationship will go cold.** It's just like a friend of yours. If you don't talk to your friend, pretty soon a week goes by and you haven't picked up the phone, and then a month goes by or a couple of months go by; pretty soon it's a few years since you've spoken with them, and you wonder what happened. It's the same thing with a customer list. If you don't continuously work to keep that relationship strong, that relationship will go bad, and the list will become useless to you because they don't treat you any differently than they do anybody else who's mailing them. You're back to square one trying to build your list again.

So you might as well spend your time cultivating that relationship by mailing to them as often as possible. Some people send email offers to their list every single day. For some people, it's several times a week by snail mail. When you're constantly in touch with your customers, that rapport is going to strengthen and they'll be more likely to buy from you. This idea that it's all a numbers game is the wrong thinking. At some level, yes, the numbers do come into play. **But what this is really a *relationship* game, so you have to do things that let people know that you *do* care about them, that you *do* have their best interest in mind.** You have to be honest with them; they all know that you're trying to get something, too, so be very clear about what's in it for you. You have to address their skepticism.

And let me re-emphasize something that I always try to emphasize when I'm discussing this subject: **I feel that a lot of people don't understand the DRM business, because they think that it's somehow different than other businesses.** But it's not. Over and over, I tell people that you should think of your DRM business as restaurant. Everybody has a favorite restaurant, right? You've probably been going there several years. Everybody can understand that no restaurant ever succeeds unless it has regular customers that keep coming back again and again, with some extreme exceptions — like the ones built alongside a busy freeway or inside a mall. But for the most part, if you're not doing something to encourage your customers to return, if you're not trying to treat them right, they're going to start going to the other restaurants in town; and soon you're going to be forced to go out of business, because you just can't make enough money to keep your doors open.

Well, every business is the *same exact way*, the DRM

business included. **It's *not* different; it's exactly the same.** You've got to do a good job of serving your customers. You need to be there for them, trying to understand why they buy what they buy, trying to get behind their eyeballs, trying to have a close relationship with them... just the way you understand your friends. **You should consider your customers your friends,** in fact, and really try to understand what it is that they want the most, so that you can serve it up to them in the best possible way.

As I wrap up this chapter, let me steal a comment again from my colleague Eric Bechtold: **success leaves clues, clues that you can follow and learn from.** You don't want to reinvent the wheel, and — I can't say this enough — **you don't get rich by yourself. You don't become a good marketer by yourself, either.** You don't just sit down one day, and a light goes on and you know every single thing you need to know. You do things like you're doing right now. You read, you get on conference calls, you listen to audios, you learn from people who have what you don't have — and you fill in the blanks.

And remember how I was talking about using lures to attract customers? Many times you have multiple lures in the marketing waters. That way, when one lure isn't working, it's not like the presses stop and all the money stops coming in. **When you find a lure that's working, go out and you find another lure, and then another, and try to maintain multiple lines in the water at all times.** If one of your lures doesn't work, offer your list another. In order to do that, you've got to track who came in with what offer in your database, so you can segment out your list by whatever lure you were using at the time. This allows you to know where one lure might work better than another.

Getting your customer in the door is just step one. That's the hardest thing you have to do. **The real money is in selling**

them over and over; that's the key to success. It's much easier to sell somebody something or get them to take your desired action if they've already taken an action, because once they've taken that action, they're psychologically bonded to you. They feel comfortable. They were able to justify one purchase, so it's much easier for them now to come back and say, "Okay, this person is a good person. I've already bought a product from them and they did a good job of delivering that product, so I'm going to do it again."

That's why **you need to be constantly on the lookout for other offers, including other Joint Venture partners,** as I've mentioned previously. That means finding people who are doing the same things as you and have similar products and services. **Call them up and tell them you'd like to offer their product to your database.** If you were to call me and say, "I have 10,000 people who bought this product. It's very similar to your product line. Would you mind putting it in front of your audience base for, let's say, 70 percent of the money?" or something like that, I'd probably rise to the bait. **We entrepreneurs always need to have the next offer ready to go,** and as long as that offer is good and something my audience base would be willing to buy, you just made my life a lot easier.

It really is as simple as having a strategy for bringing in new customers and building new relationships with clients, all the while continuing to do more and more business with the people you already have on your list. **If you do those two things successfully, then not only are you continuing to feed your business with new clients, but you're maintaining the relationship you have with your existing clients.** In a way, it's like a funnel: you're always bringing in new clients, using your front-end lead generation strategy, and then building those relationships you already have with clients who have already purchased from you. If you've got that working like it should be, you'll never run out of people to sell to.

That's our marketing strategy in a nutshell. **We constantly have some new front-end promotions out there that bring us new customers automatically, and then we have as many different systems as we can juggle to re-sell those customers again and again.** We've been doing it since 1988. And yes, there's a lot to it. On one hand, all of this is very basic, very simple. On the other, there are still a lot of unanswered questions, and people get bogged down with the details. The nice thing about having formulas and systems is that it makes it so that any time you get a little confused, you can take a deep breath, relax a bit, and go back to the fundamentals so you don't become overwhelmed and frustrated.

I use the chess analogy as a way of explaining this. There are only six different types of chess pieces; and yet, if you've ever played the game, especially if you've played it with somebody who's really good... oh man, they can smoke you in three or four moves! A good chess player can beat you a hundred different ways, and they're always thinking three or four moves down the road, whereas most of us are just thinking about the next move. Business is like that, too. **There are so many simple and fundamental strategies you can use, and if you put them into play carefully and logically, you'll have a true competitive advantage over everybody else in your market.**

CHAPTER NINE:

Marketing Should Be Fun!

In order to really succeed at marketing, it has to be enjoyable to you. Don't think of it as work — at least, not the way most people think of work. To them, work is a nasty, dirty, filthy, rotten four-letter word. But here's a good four-letter word that represents what I'm talking about here: "GAME." **Think of marketing as a game, one you're playing both for fun and to win.** The goal of this game is to see how much money you can make in the fastest time. Money's how you keep score, you see. As long as you're doing it ethically, with high moral standards and lots of integrity, play it full out!

I love what I do, and I don't really consider it work. That's true of most of my colleagues. People look at me and say, "I know you put in long hours, and do so many things. How do you do that?" Well, unlike them, I'm not punching a time clock, and watching time tick by, waiting for 5 PM. My days go by so fast; I sit down at my desk, I look up, and the day is over. **It's a rush, and I'm *excited* to work every single day.** I'm excited to play the game, and it's all about fun.

Now, I'll admit that most of us entrepreneur types aren't the types of people who watch sports or have passionate hobbies and do many things that monopolize their leisure time. **I've gotten to the point now where during my leisure time, I'm**

still learning this stuff. Eventually, as you start doing it more and more, it becomes more of a passion; even in your off time, you're going to be looking over marketing books and trying to come up with new ideas, because the more ingrained you get in the game, the more you just want to play it. **You become a student of the game;** I think this is where my chess analogy is a perfect one. You can't be a master chess player if you're a weekend park player, sitting there punching that little clock. Master chess players play every day for hours, against both live people and computers. They're constantly focused on honing their mind, honing the systems. But again, going back to what I said in the last chapter, **it all starts from just sitting down and learning the rules and fundamentals, about how you can move the different pieces.** You can learn that in a few minutes, right? **But mastering it takes a lifetime.** The more and more you digest it, and the more you spend time trying to get better and better, the more you're going to become addicted to it. With marketing, you'll eventually become a junkie of sorts, addicted to your game.

And that's part of the secret to any veteran marketer's success. The real difference between most business owners and most entrepreneurs is that entrepreneurial people like you and I tend to think of marketing as a game, pure and simple. Unfortunately, many small business owners lose sight of that. **To them, their business is more of a job, something that they do — whereas, with us it's a part of who we are.**

Every day I look forward to working in my office, talking at seminars and workshops, and meeting with my staff to decide what we should do next. And that's good, not just because it breeds enthusiasm but because the whole process simply isn't as easy you might think it is. Now, I'm not saying that difficulty is a bad thing, just that succeeding at business isn't something magical, even if you *do* make it a game. **It does take some**

effort and thought, and you have to make sure that you're following certain sequences, formulas, and systems. But then, that's why it's important that you consider it a game. As with chess, even though the basics are easy, it can take a lifetime to master before you become one of those guys who can think 14 moves ahead. **But it's still something that's very doable for anybody of normal intelligence and ability.** If you have an honest desire to make more money, you'll be able to go out there and master the game. Will it take years? Yes, but you'll learn a lot, and have so much fun along the way.

That's especially easy if you fall in love with it. One of my favorite quotes is, **"If you love something enough, it will reveal its secrets to you."** Somebody who's a lot smarter than me said that back in the 1700's or 1800's. What that means to me is that the more you fall in love with this game of turning small amounts of money into a fortune, and learning all of the marketing tips, tricks, and strategies that you have to in order to do that, then you're taking something that can be very difficult and making it a hell of a lot of fun.

CHAPTER TEN

Marketing
The Back-End

❖

I want to kick this chapter off by talking about why your desire to make easy money is both your worst enemy and your best asset. You see, most of us are kind of lazy when it comes to putting what we know into practice. A lot of people just want to learn the bare bones about marketing, so they can put a sales letter together, send it out, and then sit back and pull millions of dollars out of their mailbox. That's the way a lot of people view DRM.

The truth is, that's just ridiculous. I'm not going to pull any punches here: you're a serious student of marketing and want to really know how this works, or you wouldn't be reading this book, now would you? **You need to realize that almost all the profits in this business of information marketing come from the back-end** — which is literally the tail end of any marketing process, about as far from cobbling together a sales letter as you can get. You can't just sit there and write a letter to people you don't have any affinity with, who don't know who you are, and expect them to start throwing money at you hand over fist. Now, there's a time and a place for that; those big pay days happen, but you need to realize that they happen on the back-end.

Let's break it down. There are two different types of offers: front-end and back-end. **Front-end offers are what you use to**

develop your customer base. No matter what industry you're in, that's what you're actually using to pull in your clients to begin with. Those are your new customer acquisition offers, your lead generation. Frankly, **you're going to spend about 20% percent of your time and effort on getting new customers in the front door. Eighty percent of your time is going to be working with existing customers, because again, that's where most of your money is made: on the back-end.**

One way to illustrate this is to think about it as that sales funnel everybody talks about, where you're bringing people in and building rapport. Your offer could be something low-cost or free, just to get them in the door: a loss leader item, as they call it in retail. **Even if you lose money on it, you capture their information, add them to a direct-mail campaign, and start to build a relationship with those people.** This is applicable to a retail environment or anything else, too, but my expertise is in DRM, so that's how I prefer to explain it. Let's say my front-end right now is a $20 offer. We get people to pay us $20, and we really deliver on that. We give them a lot of great stuff so that they're excited about it, and that's part of building that rapport.

But again, most wannabes want to just write a letter, sit back, and have money come pouring in. **That's not going to happen, typically, which is the reason that it's your worst enemy.** The only time it happens is when you've been playing the game long enough, and you've built up the front end and acquired a database of people who are now excited about what it is you have to share with them. **Again, there's that "stored energy"** I talked about several chapters ago, a wonderful phrase I stole from my friend Eric Bechtold. Remember when you were a little kid and had one of those little balsa wood airplanes that had a little rubber band engine? You could sit there and wind it and wind it and wind it, and when you let it go, it would fly! But it took effort to get that stored energy in place, right? That's like your database, your list of customers. Once you've developed that list, any time you want to make money, you've got a group of people you can make other offers to. You've already "wound them up."

In addition to being your worst enemy, that desire to make easy money is also your best asset, if you're in the business of providing people with business opportunities and moneymaking solutions. **It really helps you understand what people are excited about; it helps you get into the mind of your consumer, so that you can then position other offers.** This is something to think about when you're trying to develop your front-end offers: **Think about what it is you can sell on the back-end. That front-end offer exists primarily to qualify people.** It needs to define those people, so that you can use that knowledge to understand what they want to spend money on. This, in turn, tells you what they're truly passionate about. Get in the minds of those people, and you can marry other offers to their desires.

The fact that you like easy-money solutions helps put you in the shoes of your prospects. **You can think about what type of offers would appeal to you, what you would be looking for if you were on the other side of the cash register. This puts you in the position of making huge profits on the back-end,** assuming you're willing to put this knowledge into play. You shouldn't think about jumping into this game and then get frustrated if your front-end is going a little slower than you imagined. That tells you something right there. It's not like you can just send out a little flyer, and all of a sudden all the money in the world is coming in. It takes a little time and mastery to get that database put together so that you can generate those big back-end pay days once you get the ball rolling.

At M.O.R.E., Inc., we call the front-end product the "gateway" product, because it's a good way of thinking about it. That's all it is: a gateway. Part of the secret is that you've got to blow people's minds. **You've got to get them so excited that when they get that front-end gateway package, they're so impressed they can't wait to see what you'll offer them next.** There are so many marketers out there who don't get that and never will — and thank God, because it makes it easier to compete! They'll send somebody something for $20-30, but they'll spend as little as possible on that item, so that when people get it, they're hopelessly disappointed. That leads to very few back-end sales.

We prefer to just pile on the quality; in fact, we'll often spend more on a front-end offer than we could possibly get for it. Remember Christmas when you were a kid? Remember how you couldn't wait, and you opened the packages up and you had such great gifts? It was exciting! So we try to put a lot of stuff into our packages so when people open it up they go, "Holy crap! I can't believe they gave me all of this stuff!" And then we start trying to do things to build that relationship even faster.

One of our current gateway packages is based on a model we're using to create more just like it. Now, I'm not exaggerating when I say that **what we're trying to do, as a rule of thumb, is offer to give people $1,000 worth of value for every $10 that they spend.** We're doing that by including certificates for some of our high-priced marketing seminars and for certain coaching programs. So we're giving them real value here, blowing their minds in the process. We're making a great impression. Think of it as a first date. If you're a young man and you've found the woman that you want to marry, you're going to make sure that your car is spotless, and you'll shower, wear cologne, and put on the best clothing you own. You're going to be on your best behavior. It's the same thing when you're selling to somebody the first time. You're going to be on your very,

very best behavior, because you're trying to make a favorable impression.

So over-deliver; really go overboard. **You need to think about your gateway, your front-end product as putting your best foot forward, because it really is the start of that relationship.** It's the little "seed" that's going to grow, and that's very important to get right. A lot of people think of selling something on the back-end, and want to do something really mediocre on the front-end. Well, that doesn't set the stage for a back-end sale. It just sets the stage for that person to think your next offer is going to be just as cheap as the first one. **So you really don't want to consider your front-end offer as a moneymaking situation for you; there's a time to make money, and it's on the back-end.** You want to think of that front-end as the wooing stage.

Having Affairs with Hot Products

Let's look at that relationship analogy again. I've got another good tip for you: Discover how having affairs with hot products can make you millions. **What I mean by that is this: When you're making a front-end offer, consider involving yourself with other people's offers.** Many of the entrepreneurs I know actually sell other people's products as well as anything they create internally; in fact, **in many cases their primary source of income is other people's products.** They like to get involved with other people's offers and promote their offers because, really, you can spend a lot of time and effort falling in love with products and going down the wrong road, developing product lines and putting all your effort and money into projects that nobody's really going to care about other than you. **A lot of people make that horrible mistake of falling in love with a product, when they should be falling in love with the marketplace and *then* figuring out a way to give that market**

what they want.

So discover how to have affairs with hot products! You need to get excited about the different markets out there, the different things people are excited about; **keep your finger on the pulse, and always look to what people are buying already.** Again, you don't want to try to predict the future; you want to find out what people are already excited about. That's why I use the word "affair," because it can be hot one day and cool off the next day. If you fall in love, that suggests you're going to have a long-term commitment, whereas if you're having an affair, it can be like a little fling. It can be something you get involved in, you work with it, and as soon as it starts to cool off you can keep your eyes on the horizon for the next fling, the next thing you're going to get involved in.

A lot of people don't understand this; they're always looking for what they call "a home," something they can hang their hat on for 10 or 20 years. **And there _are_ certain marketplaces that have that type of longevity, but most marketplaces don't.** They fall into the life-cycle of a bell curve, and of course there are product life cycles. It starts when your product is brand new and just being introduced, and people are just starting to use it. Then it goes through a growth phase where it's starting to increase, and more and more people out there know about it. Then it gets to a maturity stage. It's like the lifecycle of a human: you're born, you're a baby, you grow, and you mature — and then you slowly get older, and you start to decline. It happens in every industry, with every product. You need to realize that you don't want to hang your hat onto something that has a cycle like this for so long that you're married to it — so that when it starts to die off , that's the only thing you can think about. **You need to realize that you want to have affairs with markets while they're hot, because what's current creates currency, and what's hot today might**

not be hot tomorrow. You don't want to fall in love with something and become so committed to it that when the next hot thing comes along, you just say, "Oh no, I'm working on this thing. I can't possibly look at something else," because then you find yourself in a situation where that hotter thing, which could have produced a lot more revenue for you because it's more current, passes you by — and you're stuck with something that may be on the decline, so that you're losing out on a lot of big opportunities.

This point interrelates with what we were talking about earlier, **because your front-end offers should always be built around these hot marketplaces.** New things are also like magnets, in that they pull people in and get them engaged because they want to know what's new and what's exciting and what's next. That's exactly what you're providing them by doing that. **And, again, a lot of people make the mistake of sticking with one thing.** I've talked to people who say, "Oh, I've been doing this for five years." I ask, "Well have you made any money?" And the reply is, "Um... I made a little bit in the beginning, and I've really just stuck with it." That's a mistake. If you're not making more and more money as time goes by with a particular product or opportunity, then at the very least you need to be a little "untrue" to it and dabble in a hotter market or better offer.

Fall in love with your market; *don't* **fall in love with your products or services.** We say this to people all the time, and it always seems to shock them, because they just don't understand the game. We tell them that products are a dime a dozen — and really they are. **The product itself is not nearly as important as getting inside the hearts and the minds of the people you want to sell to.** That's why I have to say this one more time (and I hope I'm not sounding too much like a broken record): **you've got to find a hot market that you have**

some affinity with. The business opportunity market is the market I think you they should be focusing on if you're a business opportunity enthusiast, as so many of my clients are. It takes one to know one, as the old cliché goes.

You want to fall in love with the people that you sell to. **The more that you can really fall in love with them, and the more they're your friends, the higher the profits.** You have to think of people that you work with as your friends, and you have to treat them as your friends. **It's all about relationships.** We say that so often, but there are so many people who've just never figured it out. They think it's all just about the money, and that's all they care about. **There are a lot of aggressive, unethical marketers out there, and I try to stay away from them.** Sure, they're playing the game I talked about in the last chapter; but sadly, their game isn't based on trying to treat people with any respect. All they want to do is get as much money as they can as fast as they can, and keep as much of it as they can. They're out there raping and pillaging. And yes, at first some of those guys do make a lot of money. Most of the time, they also end up with serious legal problems — and other problems. They all seem to have problems with other relationships in their lives, too.

I'm not trying to come across like I'm holier than thou, but we've always viewed our customers as friends. **We try to treat people with dignity and respect, show them appreciation, and make them feel important** — because they *are*! These are the people providing you with food, shelter, and riches. We're not playing some manipulative game, trying to trick our customers into feeling important. That's nonsense, because making them feel important shouldn't be hard. They *are* important, and that's why you're treating them that way. Those attitudes rub off, and people can sense that. Now, I'll admit there are some seasoned con men (and women) who do a good job of faking it, but eventually people find them out. It's all about loving people, treating people with respect, trying to give them tremendous value. **When they're not happy you're not happy, and you're trying to do everything possible to right that wrong — even if it's not your fault.** That's just practicing good old-fashioned business, the way it was done 150 years ago, isn't it?

In order to better serve the customer, you have to get their attention in the first place. If you want to expand the audience base you have to work with, it should make sense that you want to dangle the most powerful product in front of them that you can, because that's what's going to be the "bait," if you will, the lure that gets them in and gets them to pay attention. **This is a world where there's so much "noise" out there in terms of competition.** Imagine yourself in front of a huge auditorium full of thousands of people, and they all have something they want to sell you, and they're all yelling at you. All you hear is the roaring crowd, and you can't possibly pick one out. Well, if somebody has something that really captures your attention, maybe they can hold it up or get your attention, so that you're paying attention to that person. You're focused on them. It's as if they pulled you out of that stadium and put you into a little side room, and now they're communicating with you one-on-one. You're paying attention. That's how you have to handle your customers. **You have to have hot offers, things that will almost literally *force* them to pay attention.** Put yourself on the other side of the cash register. How would they feel in this situation? What are they going to pay attention to? What's in it for them?

If somebody else has a better offer than you, or something more exciting that appeals to them more, they're probably going to be paying attention to that other person. You've got to have something that demands attention, so that you can start forging those relationships; and you have to be introduced to those people before you can build a relationship. **The customer is**

always the most important thing to us, so we're trying to take care of them and be respectful to them. Part of this process is searching for hot offers that will continue to attract new customers so that you can build and build.

Developing Great Messages

I've talked about the fact that there's a lifecycle for products, and how to find a front-end offer, and the difference between front-end offers and back-end offers. Now I'd like to talk about developing great sales messages. **Doing so is a process, not an event.** And again, this is the no-punches-pulled bare bones truth here; I'm trying to give you the nuts and bolts you really need. You need to understand that those of us basing our marketing on direct-mail aren't miracle people who just have all the answers handed to us. We weren't just born with all the knowledge we ever need to make money. **This is a process; it takes work, and it takes thinking, and it takes *re*-thinking.** It takes some brainstorming to develop great ideas.

Thomas Edison put it best when he said, "Genius is 99% perspiration and 1% inspiration." That's what I meant when I said that products and offers are a dime a dozen. **It's making them work that's hard.** That's where all the elbow grease and perspiration come in. **Again, I want you to realize that I started exactly where you are at.** We took some ideas and started thinking about our marketplace. We figured out what they wanted, and then went out and we found a hot offer — something that would match up with the desire that already existed in the marketplace — and we wrote out a sales letter and put that into the marketplace to see if we got a good result. If we got a good result, then heck, we went ahead and produced more and put *them* out there. That's something you need to realize; **you test and you re-invest and you continue to build.** You "cheat on" your products with new, hotter products if you need to. It's hard work. None of this stuff happens just by waving a magic wand and saying, "There it is — all the money you ever want is pouring in now." It does take preparation and perspiration and a little bit of inspiration. **But mostly, it's about taking the time to do it.**

The general idea of this book is to hopefully rewire your brain a bit, and make you better understand the reality of the situation. Because this isn't all just about making easy money. If all you want to do is sit in your La-Z-Boy and have money come to the front doorstep, that's not reality. Sure, it *can* happen if you've already done something to put a process into action; maybe you get residual revenue from something you did a long time ago. But even that took effort, desire, careful planning, and thinking and testing to create. **You're never going to make real money without putting effort in first. And then, realize this, too: you're just not going to find something that's going to produce forever.** I wish you could, but I haven't found one yet that I could just hang my hat on and knew that it was going to work as well tomorrow as it does today. So you always need to be thinking about what's next, how you can get positioned for the next big thing, and continue this process.

It's like a roller coaster. You get a good offer out there, and it has its peaks and its valleys; but eventually, it's going to come back into the station, its potential spent. You need to be prepared for that; **you need to always be looking out to the horizon to find another thing you can plug into.** But you're never going to get on that roller coaster in the first place until you start thinking about an offer, putting things on paper, and getting in the front of your audience so you can deliver your sales message, however you want to do that. You've got to get it out there in order to get results. **You've got to take that desire, wrap a system around it, and go out there and make this stuff *work*.**

So again, developing great selling messages is a process, not an event. **And once you do start making money, that's when things really do come together for you.** So many times we find people struggling before they hit it big. I have a friend who spent a good 10-15 years struggling, and now he's making so much money it's not even funny. We're happy for him. He's getting rich. For the longest time he was struggling and now, all of a sudden, the money is flowing in like water from an open fire hydrant. There's no stopping him now. I tell you this to illustrate the fact that what comes in so effortlessly now was once such a struggle for him. **You get better at crafting great sales messages as you go along.** It does get easier, once you're privy to the secrets. For example, **here's one we make a lot of use of: recycling.**

It's so simple. Sure, you do keep coming up with new stuff; but unfortunately the market changes quickly, and the best customers in the market are always limited to some degree. So you have to roll with the changes. **One way to do that is turn to what's worked for you before, and retool it. Add some twists, work in some new material, repackage it, and offer it to your customers.** For example: we recently had a promotion we called the IAMS-5 promotion, because it's the fifth generation of the promotion. The clients know it as something else. Each generation has looked different from the outside; but at its core it's the same basic premise. It's one way that we continue to find new ways to incorporate the things that worked the very best for us in the past again and again because, you see, **while the market does change to a degree, the people within it really don't change much.** Human nature really hasn't changed significantly in thousands of years. **People are still affected by two primary emotions, fear and greed.** It's been that way since the beginning of recorded history. It's nice to know that the market that you serve doesn't change that much.

When crafting your message to your market, you have to keep in mind what they're really excited about — and that's something usually know as a "magic bullet" or "magic pill." **You need to realize that everybody out there is looking for some sort of cure or solution that fixes their problem yesterday — the miracle cure, the instant solution.** People will throw money at you if they believe that your offer is that one solution to all their ills, real or perceived. Considering all that noise out there in the marketplace, magic bullets or magic pills are very important.

But the only use for a magic bullet is to put it into your gun, okay? You need to realize that a lot of people are out there playing to the fact that they have a solution to whatever ails you. **What they're doing is going out and researching the marketplace, figuring out what the worst pain or the worst problem is within the market, and then just writing their headline: "**We finally have a solution to "X"!" Right? Think about those diet pills on TV you're going to see all over the place around New Year's : "Just take this pill and the fat will magically drip off your body." They're never going to say, "Take this pill, and with a diet and exercise you'll lose weight," now are they? Sure, that's probably what the actual bottle says when it comes. But the magic bullet marketing out there will just say, "Take this and you'll watch the fat melt off your body."

And you need to realize that magic bullets do exist, but just like those miracle drugs on TV, they usually come with that long list of crazy side effects. Magic bullet advertising strategies are effective when you're playing to the pain of the customer base, because it's a good way to overcome all that noise in the marketplace. **But you need to make sure you tell them about the magic bullet, and then when they make that purchase, you give them *everything* they need in order to overcome that problem.** You have to provide what you're claiming to provide.

You can't just tell them you've got a solution if you actually don't. **You can make promises, but make sure that your marketing can back that up.** The idea, again, is to create an offer that really plays to people's pain, then that gives them the solution they're looking for, because they're going to throw money at you if you can do that. You want to come at them with something that they feel is the ultimate solution, exactly what they've been looking for.

So when you're out there in the marketplace, take the time to dig in and study those headlines that really capture your attention. Flip through the magazines that are playing to your marketplace. If you're an automotive buff and you want to sell to other automotive buffs, go through the automobile magazines. If you're interested in guns, look to *Guns & Ammo*. If you're interested in business opportunities, go to *Entrepreneur*, *Home Business Connection,* or *Home Business Journal.* **Analyze those headlines that pull you in right off the bat, and normally you'll find a magic bullet — something that stops you dead in your tracks, that plays to your pain.** It makes you want to buy that product, because it's something that's really been agitating you for a long time. "How am I going to solve that? Oh well, I'll just buy that product and I'll feel all better."

We often talk about how "the more things change, the more they remain the same." And yes, we're living in a fast-changing world; but it's always comforting to know that human nature doesn't change. **People want easy answers; and if anything, we're getting lazier than ever.** Most people claim they want to make more money, but they're never going to listen to a moneymaking program. They're not going to take even the slightest bit of action. **They want somebody to do everything for them.** The companies that are providing those kinds of services are making money faster than they can spend it. And you know what? You might as well be one of those people. **Offer to**

do things for people; let them know you'll just take care of it for them. That's always been a good tactic, but again, it's getting more and more common in every market. That's the basis of this magic bullet concept. But remember this: **the magic bullet also works for people who *aren't* lazy.** I have some friends in Utah who sell a high-dollar coaching program. Their clients are extremely busy, and extremely successful; and one of their top-selling services is something that handles a very important thing on behalf of the client. And it's not that they're lazy; they're overwhelmed. They've got too much to do already, so they can't handle this particular thing. What they have is a lot of money to spend, so they're more than happy to give it to our friends.

The point is, in every single market you've got people who, for whatever reason, just want you to take care of everything, because you've got a proven track record and they know they can depend on you. **People are looking for somebody else to take the reins.** That's why there are so many people who are providing fast, easy solutions to those kinds of things. **Consumers always want things easier, faster, simpler, and they respond to things that promise them that.** It's an emotional thing. If our competitors are using that method and we're not, then we're losing money by not also having products and services designed to make life much easier for people.

Smart entrepreneurs take things that are extremely complicated, things that they've developed and perfected over the years, and offer to do it all for their clients. That provides them with a lot of value. But there's one little thing I need to talk about that's important in making that process work: **transparency.** One of the ways you can establish yourself as an expert in selling "we do it all for you" processes is to be very transparent with the people you're working with. **You have to go painstakingly through every little detail of how you do something, why you do it, and what the next step is.** You can even build in ways for people to check and balance the system, so they can see it all happening. These are all things that make it easy for people to feel comfortable with that process.

A lot of people try to sell "we do it all for you" programs to people without ever really being transparent, thereby showing people that they know what they're talking about. There are a lot of consultants out there, in various industries, that take you through all these crazy processes and diagrams and say, "Now, you can do this yourself — or you can just hire me. I'll come into your office and put all this stuff into action for you." **They're establishing their credibility by being transparent,** by showing you that what they're talking about isn't just a bunch of fluff and BS, but the real deal, and then offering the "we do it all for you" magic bullet on the back-end. **That's really one of the keys to our success.**

A good way to roll out an offer and attract new clients is to sell them the magic bullet concept on the front-end, where you're a bit vague about what it is you're going to do for them. You tell them how you have all the answers, and get them to request a package of information or attend a tele-seminar, where you can then go into all the details and establish your credibility so that they understand why and how this magic bullet does exist, and how you can actually fulfill the promises you're making. And then at the very end you say, "Of course, I just gave you everything you need to get from Point A to Point B. You can take that information, roll up your sleeves, and go to work. Or use me as the solution to your problem... here's where to sign." **Again, you've got to really take that work and knowledge and roll them together effectively in order to reach the people that you're trying to serve.** The neat thing about this type of offer is that, as I've mentioned, you can put the work, effort, and development in one time and sell that magic bullet a thousand times. **Re-package it, and just**

continue to roll it out there. That's one of the things I love more than anything else about this information marketing industry. The pain and effort goes into something once when you create it, and then you continue to benefit from it, sometimes for years to come. That's very powerful.

So how do you go about doing it all for someone? Here's another analogy that I think works pretty well. Let's assume you're selling trash service, something we all need. I can come to you and say, "Okay, we're a new trash service here and we're replacing your old service. Here's what we offer: We'll pick up your trash at the curb in the fancy little receptacle we provide you. We'll put it into our truck and haul it to the trash station, where we'll weight it in. We'll put it into the trash bin there and we'll pay our ongoing trash fees that we have to pay in order to use the dump. Then we'll hose off our trucks and clean everything out. We'll pay our employees to do the same thing over and over again every Thursday for you, and all you do is you pay a little fee. Or, here's how you get your permits to go get rid of it the dump. You have to take the trash in every Thursday yourself. You don't have any receptacles, so you have to provide those as well as haul your own garbage. Here's the phone number and the address where you need to go. Here's everything you need to do, all the painstaking details. Or hey, just pay us and we'll pick up your trash on Tuesday. It's only $100 a year to do that for you."

So what are you going to do? It's a weird little example, maybe, but these guys know what they're doing. They take your garbage, it magically goes away to where it's supposed to go, and you feel comfortable with that situation. You can think about any business solution the same way. **If it's something they have to get done and they can pay you to do it for them, then that will eliminate the pain, effort, and struggle it would take them to do it.** So by all means, they're going to throw money at you over and over again.

If you're going to do one of these "we do it all for you" services, **try to build it around an ongoing need.** There are plenty of angles you can incorporate into your business if you're open to this type of thinking. The answers will come to you if you take all this stuff, put it in a little mental box, then focus on it; and understand, of course, that a lot of these things are going to take you some time to develop. **But once they're in place, you can just turn on the faucet and money will come pouring out for years to come.**

Along the way, you'll always learn new things. We've been doing this since 1988, and we're still finding new ways to do what we've been doing for years. **You never really run out of ideas. In fact, our goal is twofold:** NUMBER ONE, we want to think new thoughts we've never thought before, so we can come up with new ideas we've never thought of. NUMBER TWO, we look for all the things that have worked for us in the past, and find new ways to re-purpose them. And let me re-emphasize this: it's a process, not an event. People are in a hurry to make millions of dollars, just as I one was. The funny thing is, once you start getting a few of these things in place, the money will come in so fast and so furiously you'll wonder where it was all of those years that you were struggling! Our first five years we generated more than $10,000,000 worth of DRM revenue. **Money can come in very quickly when you pair the right offer to the right market and implement it the right way.** It's just that sometimes there's a struggle; and of course there's a learning curve.

As part of that process, you must realize that you have to earn people's trust. **You have to earn their respect.** You can say that for every relationship. And yet, a lot of marketers, especially those new to the business, aren't even thinking in terms of relationships. They have no plan to build those bonds of trust with people.

The Four Stages of Learning

I want to round out this chapter (and this book) with an idea in four stages: **the stages of learning something new.** Learning can be distressing and a bit frightening, so let's go through these four stages here so that you can relax a little and come to understand that it's a natural process.

The FIRST STAGE is unconscious incompetence; basically, this is ignorance. You don't know what you don't know, so you really have no idea what's going on; you're a bit scared, and maybe you just don't even think about it. **Then there's STAGE TWO: conscious incompetence, when you begin to realize and discover the things you don't know.** This is the frustration and confusion period. You're still incompetent and ignorant about the whole thing, but at least your eyes are beginning to open, and you realize that there's a bigger world out there — that this is a game, and there are little things that you can do to make it better.

Then you've got STAGE THREE, conscious competence, where you can function in this new area, but it's a major struggle and you're not very good at it. This is where most marketers are: they're thinking about their business, and they're struggling, and they're really digging in and trying to find the best thing that they can promote and everything. **But at least they're moving forward in the right direction.** You stumble along. This is what I was talking about when I mentioned my friend who struggled for 10-15 years before he started to make lots of money. It's like one of those rock bands that becomes an overnight success, because they've been out touring and in the bar scenes for 20 years. **They just finally hit the point of unconscious competence, where they've mastered it. That's STAGE FOUR here: you get to where you do it naturally, like a duck swims.** People just say, "Oh, you're a natural — you just have this natural ability to make money." No, you've spent a lot of time and effort understanding what you didn't know. You learned how to put it to work for you, and now you can look at something and see it in a different light, and can make it happen a lot faster than most other people. **But the whole process took a long time.**

In that conscious competence stage, you can make a lot of money very quickly, and it can happen very fast. You don't have to master everything in order to play the game and in order to have some victories. But what's going to happen is, **eventually your losses, the things that you try that don't work, will start to get fewer and farther between.** This is especially the case if you treat it like a game, as I talked about in the last chapter, because when you really have a true desire to make it work and it's fun, it's the world's best addiction.

So immerse yourself in the field you're in. Listen to presentations, get new ideas, read books like this one, and try things. Don't just expect to wake up one day and have this unconscious competence, this mastery. **It takes a while.** It's like learning martial arts. Those Buddhist monks up in the Himalayan Mountains go up there as small children and come down as Kung Fu masters. They didn't walk up there one day and just say, "Hand me the pebble, Master, and make me some sort of triple black belt." It took time, commitment, and effort... but it's fun and rewarding, and along the way you get better and better, and then one day you're an overnight success. I think that's something you really need take to heart. **Understand that this can happen for you, and that you can make a whole heck of a lot of money on your road to unconscious competence — but it's a step-by-step process.** Your steps may take a little longer than others, but just keep at it, and eventually you'll get to that point where you're a marketing master.

It's all part of the game.

www.ingramcontent.com/pod-product-compliance
Lightning Source LLC
Chambersburg PA
CBHW022111210326
41521CB00028B/217

* 9 7 8 1 9 3 3 3 5 6 3 0 3 *